Engaging
the Bible

Critical Readings from Contemporary Women

Edited by

Hee An Choi

and

Katheryn Pfisterer Darr

Fortress Press
Minneapolis

ENGAGING THE BIBLE
Critical Readings from Contemporary Women

Unless otherwise noted, Scripture quotations are from the New Revised Standard Version Bible, copyright © 1989 by the Division of Christian Education of the National Council of the Churches of Christ in the USA and used by permission.

Scripture quotations marked KJV are from the King James Version Bible.

Cover image: "Rejoice maiden, unbound!" © 2005, Kelly Rider
Cover and book design: Abby Hartman

Library of Congress Cataloging-in-Publication Data

Engaging the Bible : critical readings from contemporary women / edited by Hee An Choi and Katheryn Pfisterer Darr.
   p. cm.
Includes index.
ISBN-13: 978-0-8006-3565-7 (alk. paper)
ISBN-10: 0-8006-3565-5 (alk. paper)
1. Bible—Feminist criticism. 2. Bible and feminism. 3. Bible—Criticism, interpretation, etc. I. Choi, Hee An. II. Darr, Katheryn Pfisterer, 1952-
 BS521.4.E54 2006
 220.6082—dc22
                                    2006016208

The paper used in this publication meets the minimum requirements of American National Standard for Information Sciences—Permanence of Paper for Printed Library Materials, ANSI Z329.48-1984.

Manufactured in the U.S.A.

Contents

Contributors

Hee An Choi is Lecturer and Director of the Anna Howard Shaw Center at Boston University School of Theology and author of *Korean Women and God: Experiencing God in a Multi-Religious Colonial Context* (2005).

Katheryn Pfisterer Darr is Professor of Hebrew Bible at Boston University and author of "The Book of Ezekiel: Commentary and Reflections" in *The New Interpreter's Bible*, vol. 6 (2001); *Isaiah's Vision and the Family of God* (1994); (assisting Bernhard W. Anderson) *Understanding the Old Testament, 4th Abridged Edition* (1994); and *Far More Precious Than Jewels: Perspectives on Biblical Women* (1991).

Aida Irizarry-Fernández is District Superintendent for the Metropolitan Boston Hope District, New England Conference, of the United Methodist Church.

Cheryl Townsend Gilkes is John D. and Catherine T. MacArthur Professor of Sociology and program chair in African-American Studies at Colby College, Waterville, Maine, and author of *If It Wasn't for the Women: Black Women's Experience and Womanist Culture in Church and Community* (2000).

Carter Heyward is Howard Chandler Robbins Professor of Theology, emerita, at Episcopal Divinity School, Cambridge, Massachusetts, and author of *God in the Balance: Christian Spirituality in Times of Terror* (2002); *Staying Power: Reflections on Gender, Justice, and Compassion* (2001); *Saving Jesus From Those Who Are Right: Rethinking What It Means to Be Christian* (Fortress Press, 1999); and *Touching Our Strength: The Erotic as Power and the Love of God* (1989), among other titles.

Kwok Pui-lan is William F. Cole Professor of Christian Theology and Spirituality at Episcopal Divinity School, Cambridge, Massachusetts; author of *Postcolonial Imagination and Feminist Theology* (2005), *Introducing Asian Feminist Theology* (2000), and *Discovering the Bible in the Non-Biblical World* (1995); and co-editor of *Beyond Colonial Anglicanism* (2001).

Elisabeth Schüssler Fiorenza is Krister Stendahl Professor of Divinity at Harvard Divinity School, Cambridge, Massachusetts; author of *Wisdom Ways: Introducing Feminist Biblical Interpretation* (2001), *Jesus and the Politics of Interpretation* (2000), *Rhetoric and Ethic: The Politics of Biblical Studies* (Fortress Press, 1999), *Sharing Her Word: Feminist Biblical Interpretation in Context* (1998), *Bread Not Stone: The Challenge of Feminist Biblical Interpretation*, 10th anniversary edition (1995), *In Memory of Her: A Feminist Theological Reconstruction of Christian Origins*, 10th anniversary edition (1994), *Jesus: Miriam's Child, Sophia's Prophet: Critical Issues in Feminist Christology* (1994), and *But She Said: Feminist Practices of Biblical Interpretation* (1992); and editor of *Searching the Scriptures: A Feminist Introduction*, 2 vols. (1997), among other titles.

Introduction

Hee An Choi

The United States of America is a nation of immigrant people, and the country bears a long and painful immigration history. Prior to the seventeenth century, North America was populated by various tribes of native peoples. During the seventeen and eighteenth centuries, colonizers, primarily European, immigrated to this continent. These colonizers brought African people here by force in order to exploit their labor.

In the twentieth century, nine million immigrants entered the United States. Over the past ten to fifteen years, an additional ten million immigrants have arrived, the largest wave in U.S. history. Before 1990, most immigrants came from Europe and Canada; since 1990, the largest number has come from Asian countries. Statisticians tell us that over the next five to ten years, Spanish-speaking people will become the largest ethnic group in the United States.

Signs of these demographic shifts are all around us. Ethnic restaurants thrive not only in major metropolitan areas but also in small towns. Radio stations play traditional and contemporary music, and television and movie screens display images from around the world. More persons of color are visible and influential in sports, business, government and politics, and entertainment than ever before.

Many Christian churches are discovering that their neighborhoods have a look and feel different than they did in the more monocultural eras in which they were founded. How does the church serve persons in these changed and ever-changing settings? How do Christian pastors and lay persons perceive, interpret, and interact with other people in these increasingly multicultural environments? How do shifting circumstances affect our efforts to communicate Christ's message to others? How do they influence our interpretations of biblical texts?

From 2003 to 2004, programming sponsored by the Anna Howard Shaw Center (cosponsored by the Center for Congregational Research and Development) at Boston University School of Theology focused especially on multiculturalism. This programming included "A Mosaic of Voices," a multicultural lecture series.

At the Shaw Center's invitation, five women theologians representing different cultural, ethnic, and/or social perspectives (African American, Asian/Asian American, Latina/Hispanic, Caucasian, and straight and lesbian) presented two-part lectures to gatherings of ordained and lay women and men, students, and professors. In their lectures, these theologians explored the diverse contexts of Christian ministry and different methodological approaches to interacting with Scripture. Bible study participants, in turn, raised their own voices in a culturally diverse chorus.

This volume is a concrete expression of the Anna Howard Shaw Center's desire to share our Bible study experiences with a wider audience. Readers will encounter a wealth of cultural, ethnic, and social contexts within which biblical interpretation springs to life. The essays in *Engaging the Bible* illustrate how we can better equip ourselves, our churches, and our communities to raise multicultural consciousness and to broaden and enrich the interpretive strategies by which we bring our own struggles and experiences into dialogue with biblical traditions.

Each lecture consisted of an introduction concerned with method in biblical interpretation followed by an applied contextual analysis of selected biblical texts. In Part 1 of her essay, Cheryl Townsend Gilkes introduces readers to Afro-Christian oral traditions, Negro spirituals, and African-American cultural imagination and biblical interpretation. She explores how prayers, testimonies, music, and sermons reflect the religious experiences of African Americans and their uses of the Bible in everyday life.

From an Asian/Asian American woman's perspective, Kwok Pui-lan shares her struggle with colonialism in America, analyzing the relationship between national politics and its religious justifications in the United States from the perspective of postcolonial studies. She illustrates how intersections of gender, sexuality, and national politics play out in the United States and how they affect women of color in the United States and women in the Third World.

Aida Irizarry-Fernández describes the diversity of Latino cultures and their contributions to Latino ministerial contexts. Relating her own experience to Ezekiel's vision of the valley of dry bones (Ezek. 37:1-14), she discusses the resilience of Latino communities and their sense of identity.

Elisabeth Schüssler Fiorenza embraces a new understanding of feminism and inclusivity. Her methodological approach is a critical

Introductionix

feminist interpretation for liberation and emancipation that claims interpretive privileges for oppressed and marginalized people and offers a critical historical and religious consciousness informed by the feminist tradition of wo/men's religious authority.

Beginning with Mel Gibson's film, *The Passion of the Christ*, Carter Heyward examines different perspectives on the Bible's authority and on other religious traditions, within, and beyond North American christianity. As a lesbian feminist Christian, she responds to heterosexism in society and in the Bible, lifting up the experiences of women living faithfully in the Spirit of God.

Together, these introductory essays address different forms of social discrimination and oppression, illuminating the complex links joining women's unique, yet common, struggles, the Bible, and biblical interpretation. Contributors seek to connect cultural sexism with racial discrimination, classism, sexual politics, post-colonialism, and political subjugation, analyzing how these inter-related forms of oppression shape women's lives.

In Part 2 of their essays, contributors place culturally embed-ded, historically conditioned stories of biblical figures in dialogue with the practical realities of contemporary, culturally diverse women as a starting point for reinterpreting the Bible and recon-structing today's world. Cheryl Townsend Gilkes explores the interface between the biblical story of "poor man Lazarus" and the rich man and the racial and class conflicts African Americans experience in contemporary American society. Describing the challenges created by inequalities of race, ethnicity, sexual ori-entation, gender, and physical abilities, she urges us to open our hearts to "hear Moses and the prophets" and asks us to respond to people who are poor, hungry, naked, bound, and sick.

In her postcolonial reading of "the loose woman" Rahab, Kwok Pui-lan engages the perspectives of women living in the developing world in order to highlight the political imperialism expressed in contemporary colonizing culture. On the one hand, she uses feminist methodologies to critique colonialism in Amer-ica and Asia; on the other, she critiques white feminists for co-opting Rahab, who served the Israelites at the expense of her own people.

Lifting up the Latino/Hispanic communal voice, Aida Irizarry-Fernández invites us to play an imaginative and creative Bible game she learned from her Latino community. Retelling the story of 2 Kings 2:1-14 and Mark 14:3-9 through the methodology of See—Judge—Act, she offers a way for individuals to identify their own circumstances within the biblical text.

In her critical feminist interpretation of 1 Peter, Elisabeth Schüssler Fiorenza unpacks the relationship between imperial ethos and the letter's discourse. Reflecting on our inscribed and structured racism, heterosexism, classism, and colonialism, she sets out a rhetorical critical feminist critique that exposes imperial power and its effects and guides us in developing strategies to challenge them.

Carter Heyward's discussion of biblical authority in the story of Pilate, the book of Genesis, and the letters of Paul challenges us to rethink the sexist and heterosexist ordering of gender relations and dares us to think against the text. Questioning the relationship between the Bible and biblical authority, she leads us to confront the reality of oppressive patterns in the Christian church and to expand our own understanding of faith.

These authors do not content themselves with identifying the forms of oppression inscribed in biblical texts and encoded in contemporary cultures. Rather, using their own academic and ministerial approaches, they present faithful ways to overcome forms of oppression in our lived worlds. Out of their personal methods of understanding the Bible, the contributors build bridges between academic interpretations and multicultural ministerial practices. These bridges offer new challenges to Christian leaders and students of theology and bring new visions of biblical study to multicultural ministries.

The purpose of linking these diverse voices within the present volume is to address conflict and oppression and give us transforming power to deal with these realities. Reaching out from academic and ministerial worlds to those of the laity challenges both the academy and the church.

At the end of each chapter, you will find several brief questions designed to stimulate thinking and conversation. These questions can be used by individuals but will most fruitfully engage members of small groups. We hope that in dialogue with this volume's contributors and your own interpretive communities, you will become part of a "chorus of voices" singing new songs of liberation and growth.

I. A Prophetic Apocalyptic Reading

———◆———

Resurrection in Prophetic Context

"Poor Man Lazarus" and Christian Agency
Cheryl Townsend Gilkes

———◆———

And [Jesus] said unto him, If they hear not Moses and the
prophets, neither will they be persuaded, though one rose
from the dead
—Luke 16:31 KJV

Everything now, we must assume is in our hands . . . If we
. . . do not falter in our duty now, we may be able, handful
that we are, to end the racial nightmare, and achieve our
country, and change the history of the world. If we do not
dare everything, the fulfillment of that prophecy, recreated from the bible in song by a slave, is upon us: *God gave
Noah the rainbow sign, No more water, the fire next time!*
—James Baldwin[1]

Perspective

James Baldwin used the voices of enslaved African Americans to
issue his now-classic 1963 call for African-American agency on
behalf of the nation and the world: "If we do not dare everything,
the fulfillment of that prophecy, recreated from the bible in song
by a slave, is upon us: *God gave Noah the rainbow sign, No more water,
the fire next time.*" When I first read James Baldwin's *The Fire Next
Time*, I was challenged, transformed, changed—made conscious.

1

In the book's opening essay, "My Dungeon Shook," Baldwin described his experiences and admonished his nephew—and I felt like his nephew—to understand "You can only be destroyed by believing that you really are what the white world calls a *nigger*." In his second essay, "Down at the Cross," Baldwin described the confrontation taking place between Christianity and Islam within the black community, which he characterized as a very public rejection of the philosophy of the civil rights movement by the Nation of Islam: The Nation of Islam had characterized Christianity as an escapist, racist, pie-in-the-sky religion with no relevance for "the black man in America."

Baldwin saw the struggle to transcend race as a struggle to make the love ethic supreme in the movement and society. The confrontation between African-American Christianity and African-American Islam continued after the civil rights movement achieved major goals and significantly changed the United States. After Malcolm X's transformation led him to expand his analysis of social justice problems to incorporate institutional racism and powerlessness, the voices of black nationalism became even more prominent. Indeed, both African-American disillusionment with Christianity and the discovery of a spirituality that described humanity as indisputably one under God have continued to fuel the growth of Islam among African Americans and have created, according to C. Eric Lincoln and Lawrence Mamiya, one of the most significant challenges to the black church of the early twenty-first century.[2]

Since the civil rights movement, African-American Christians, prompted by the growth of black theology and related perspectives, have emphasized prophetic Christianity. The ministry of Martin Luther King Jr., with its emphasis on social justice and the beloved community, provides the model for such Christianity, and activism with and on behalf of the oppressed is viewed as paramount by prophetic African-American Christians. There is a presumption that slave religion and "the Negro Church" have been substantially transformed. That presumption dismisses and ignores the prophetic voices of enslaved Christians and their legacy of agency and struggle. There is a failure to appreciate fully the rich prophetic emphasis in the African-American religious experience prior to the civil rights movement. I seek to correct this erasure of an important component of the "mythic" foundation of the Afro-Christian tradition in the United States.

Baldwin placed the words of what James Weldon Johnson calls our "black and unknown bards," the writers of Negro spirituals[3], at the center of his universe in 1963, when the civil rights movement became the center of this nation's "contentious politics."

My Bible study also embraces and explores Negro spirituals, in my case to highlight the importance that African Americans have assigned to certain biblical texts.

The spirituals I examine come from Luke 16:19-31, the story known traditionally as "The Rich Man and Lazarus." African Americans have endowed this text with importance in at least two spirituals. One spiritual sings simply

> Rocka my soul in the bosom of Abraham
> Rocka my soul in the bosom of Abraham
> Rocka my soul in the bosom of Abraham
> Oh rocka my soul!

The other spiritual, "I Got a Home In-a Dat Rock,"[4] is more extensive and detailed in its engagement with this story. In this spiritual, the lyrics speak specifically about "Poor man Lazarus, poor as I"; they expound upon the larger meaning of the story in a way that connects "last things" with the realities of everyday life.

That Blessed Book: African Americans and Their Bibles

This essay is part of a larger project, *That Blessed Book: The Bible and the African American Cultural Imagination*, in which I examine a selection of biblical texts prominent in African-American *orature*—the oral traditions of African peoples and the written texts that capture them.[5] I ask why these ancestors, enslaved women and men and their descendants, chose these texts and flagged them through spirituals, other (folk) musical forms, folkloric stories, sermons, prayers, and naming traditions. I argue that Africans and their descendents in the United States engaged the English Bible, especially the King James Version, affectionately known as "King Jimmy," with a critical vision shaped through their experience as slaves and their observations of the Christianity of the white people who enslaved them and supported their enslavement.

When James Baldwin announced that the United States was at a social justice crossroads, particularly in the area of race, he used the spiritual, "I Got a Home in-a Dat Rock" to make his point. He wrote, "God gave Noah the rainbow sign; He said no more water but the fire next time." The power of that rhyming vision carried me across the entire panorama of biblical faith from Genesis to Revelation. In the forty years since I first read *The Fire Next Time*, I have come to a more elaborate engagement with the biblical wisdom embedded in spirituals and other African-American orature. Part of my own faith journey has been connecting my clerical consciousness and my scholarly concerns. The sociologist in me has wanted to understand and to deconstruct—that is, historicize, contextualize, and criticize—the sources of religious agency in the African-American tradition. At the same time, the African-American minister in me has wanted to serve, celebrate, and revitalize that tradition—to foster an appreciation of the African-American religious tradition, based on apologetic knowledge.

These explorations of African-American engagement with the English Bible also represent attempts to address the lack of thick description of African-American culture, especially its religious tradition. This is a central mission of my scholarship. The experience of Christian ministry, especially that of preacher and worship leader, has heightened my appreciation for and curiosity about the African-American cultural imagination and its engagement with the Bible. The discovery, the "a-ha!" moment inspiring inquiry, occurred during Christian worship where I noticed the prominence of a biblical fragment in a traditional prayer. That moment led to my in-depth exploration of a biblical fragment, "clothed [and] in my/[his] right mind," which is prominently enshrined in the African-American prayer tradition. This led to my seeing and hearing more biblical fragments in the folk traditions and to subsequent interrogations of the reasons for their prominence in the African-American oral tradition. Ever since, I have sought to develop a dynamic model of the intersection of perception and interpretation of the Bible in African-American experience.

The Bible's introduction to African Americans is almost legendary. Henry Louis Gates calls it "the trope of the talking book."[6] In several slave narratives, black women and men described the experience of having their owners attribute their authority as slave owners and the legitimacy of what they were doing or saying to the Bible ("my Bible tells me"). Occasionally, when their masters left the room, slaves would approach the book and place their ear on its pages to ask "if the book would speak to me." Listening for the book to speak to them became an important metaphor for their questing after personal revelation, a foundation of the experiential dimension of the Afro-Christian tradition.[7]

Philosopher Mary Warnock describes "imagination" as the intersection of perception and interpretation.[8] The formation of the African-American Christian tradition possesses a mythic dimension involving the English Bible, the King James (or "Authorized") Version. Africans brought to their readings a perception grounded in elaborate and rich African religious traditions, both African Traditional Religions (ATR) and Islam. Both ATR and Islam involved highly complex cosmologies. Additionally, Islam embraced monotheism and celebrated a sacred text, the Qur'an, whose narrative was rooted in oral tradition. The interpretive dimensions were shaped not only by Africans' experiences but also by their cumulative sufferings on the Middle Passage and their enslavement by people claiming to be Christian. This confluence of experiences led to a critical faith that distinguished between what Thomas L. Webber has identified as "true religion" and "slaveholding priestcraft."[9]

My larger study explores selected biblical texts that have been highlighted in African-American oral traditions: prayers, testimonies, songs, and sermons. My overall thesis is that the African-American cultural imagination offers us a prophetic-apocalyptic reading of the English Bible. The "prophetic" aspect emphasizes justice, mercy, liberation, and human equality, while the "apocalyptic" dimension asserts and affirms the final, absolute sovereignty of a God who requires answers from us about our participation in the prophetic dimension. Contained in that prophetic-apocalyptic perspective is an ethic of perseverance— persistence, community, strength, and service—that sustains hope and manifests what is prophetic and apocalyptic.

Luke 16:14-31, the story of the rich man and Lazarus, inextricably binds the prophetic to the apocalyptic. Our enslaved ancestors used this story to tell us that there is no hope beyond this world that is not tied to our actions in this world. Our actions must demonstrate an active responsibility for and accountability to the "least of these." Within this explicit prophetic-apocalyptic framework, the story addresses the immorality of extreme inequality and issues a very dramatic challenge to people of privilege. It is clear from the lyrics of "I Got a Home in-a Dat Rock" that enslaved people saw clearly the injustice of their situation and believed that

God would hold oppressors accountable. Through the eyes of these "black and unknown bards," it is possible to reconstruct a conversation within the early African-American church about its relationship to "the law" or "Moses and the prophets," the canonical core of the Hebrew Bible.

"Between de Earth and Sky"

I got a home in-a Dat Rock, Don't you see?
I got a home in-a Dat Rock, Don't you see?
Between the earth an' sky,
Thought I heard my Savior cry,
You got a home in-a Dat Rock, Don't you see?

Poor man Lazrus, poor as I, Don't you see?
Poor man Lazrus, poor as I, Don't you see?
Poor man Lazrus, poor as I,
When he died he foun' a home on high,
He had a home in-a Dat Rock, Don't you see?

Rich man, Dives, He lived so well, Don't you see?
Rich man, Dives, He lived so well, Don't you see?
Rich man, Dives, He lived so well,
When he died he foun' a home in Hell,
He had no home in-a Dat Rock, Don't you see?

God gave Noah the Rainbow sign, Don't you see?
God gave Noah the Rainbow sign, Don't you see?
God gave Noah the Rainbow sign,
No mo' water but fire nex' time,
Better get a home in-a Dat Rock, Don't you see?

This spiritual addresses directly the story of the rich man and Lazarus. The preaching or missionary tradition taught these singers the name of the rich man, Dives; he is not named in the Bible. The song begins with Jesus "between the earth and sky," and thus points to a crucified and resurrected Jesus. Taking seriously the faithfulness with which spirituals and other oral traditions used the words of these texts, hearing the Savior "cry" seems to be a clear reference to the crucifixion. When one takes this spiritual as part of the same tradition that sings, "Jesus is a rock in a weary land . . . a shelter in the time of storm," we hear the important fusion of persons that also occurs in the African-American tradition. The spiritual assures that Jesus includes the singer in his redemptive suffering. (The statement to the thief, "This day, thou shalt be with me in Paradise," may also be echoed here.)

The lyrics provide more evidence that suffering Christians are included in the redemptive acts of God. "Poor man Lazarus" was "poor as I." Enslaved singers saw themselves in the poor man laid at the gate. Tragically for him, he was laid at the gate of a rich man. The people were in view of one another and potentially in relationship. Furthermore, the rich man had the resources to help. Yet Lazarus was allowed to lie at the rich man's gate and die!

With no one to care for him, God sent the angels to carry Lazarus to Abraham's bosom. In "Rocka my soul in the bosom of Abraham . . . Oh! Rocka my soul!" African Americans took this singular reference to Abraham's bosom very seriously. The song is usually sung in a celebratory manner and has been incorporated into the signature dance, "Revelations," performed by the Alvin Ailey dance troupe. Only one reference to "Abraham's bosom" occurs in the entire King James Version, at Luke 16:22. Nonetheless, the story of the rich man and Lazarus has become an important component of the community's canon—those biblical texts that the community generally agrees are important—texts that are emphasized repeatedly during worship and at other community gatherings.

The spiritual "A Home in-a Dat Rock" criticizes "Dives," "the rich man." This man, too, died and "was buried." He had plenty of people to care for him. While the Bible describes him as being "in torment," our singers say more pointedly, "he foun' a home in Hell!" The point that he is "in torment" is connected both to Matthew 25 and to Rev. 14:10-11, with its threat of "everlasting fire." Not only do our bards point to the torment, they also appeal to God's promise in Gen. 9:15, where God tells Noah, "I will remember my covenant which is between me and you and every living creature of all flesh: and the waters shall no more become a flood to destroy all flesh." One can take this reference as an admonition to take the whole story seriously.

"A Home in-a Dat Rock" points out the importance of personal accountability and responsibility in *this life* for consequences in the afterlife. It points less to God as deliverer, although Lazarus eventually ends up in paradise entirely by divine action, than to

God as judge calling people to participate in the distribution of justice and the uplifting of poor brothers and sisters. This point is elaborated in "Moses and the prophets."

If They Hear not Moses and the Prophets

One of the hallmarks of the Afro-Christian tradition is the absence of a wall separating the Old and New Testaments. While most observers have emphasized the importance African Americans place on the Exodus story, these observers have not paid as much attention to the intercalation of the Old and New Testaments throughout the mythic dimension of Afro-American Christianity. Moses, Joshua, and Ezekiel have been emphasized about equally with Paul and Silas, the blind man by the road, and the women around Jesus.

"Moses" includes not only the Exodus story but the entire Torah, with its description of the jubilee—a demand for liberation and a return to equitable land distribution. The Torah contains other demands for justice for slaves and poor people, as well as just management of wealth. God's people are admonished not to harvest their fields so completely that nothing is left for the poor to harvest for themselves.

The prophets, from the point of view of early Christians and their ancient Israelite ancestors, include not only the great writing prophets but the stories found in Joshua, Judges, 1-2 Samuel, and 1-2 Kings. These, too, are used liberally throughout the song, preaching, and story-telling traditions of African Americans.

Because of the distinctive direction towards which the African American biblical imagination points, I believe that Luke 16 can be seen as legitimizing Christian appropriation of the prophetic tradition and as mediating the relationship between Christians and the law. It is popular for evangelical Christians to juxtapose Christian faith with a highly stereotyped view of the law. Yet when one takes seriously the Christian texts in which Jesus talks about the durability of the law, or, in this case, of Moses and the prophets, Christians are challenged to do better than the Pharisees (see Matt. 5:20).

Rejecting any wall separating the Testaments, enslaved African-American Christians challenge us to be prophetic Christians. The prophetic Christian is one whose relationship with the law, mediated by the emphasis on justice, erases restrictions on membership in the people of God. Paul's letters and Acts make clear that circumcision and conversion to Judaism are not prerequisites for inclusion in the body of Christ. Jesus's willingness to call sinners to what enslaved Christians called "the welcome table" makes clear that people whom the law excluded from service in the sanctuary and often from the entire community—women, people with leprosy, people with physical disabilities—are nonetheless called to membership in the church, among the people of God.

Paul's confrontations with Judaizers (for example, Galatians) and his disputation on the law as a bondwoman in Romans reflected an important argument that made it possible for "God fearers" and Gentiles to partake fully in their churches without shame about their origins. To illustrate the relationship between Jews and Gentiles in the church at Rome, I often use the example of contemporary churches in which there are church mothers who have practically memorized the Bible, are skilled worship leaders, and are able to raise songs that set congregations on fire. These extremely skilled Christians, whose mothers and grandmothers were also pillars of the church, can intimidate new Christians to the point where the new people are reluctant to participate fully as leaders and shapers of the life of the church.

The Gospel traditions, on the other hand, supply correctives to the temptation to appropriate Paul in ways that diminish the importance of the Hebrew Scriptures or dismiss them as the law. The Gospels portray a Messiah who argues constantly with the Pharisees and the Sadducees but who eventually develops very strong alliances with certain Pharisees, while Sadducees disappear from the scene. The Gospels tell us that Jesus was crucified and rose from the dead and that he lived and carried out a ministry we are called to emulate. For Paul, the mere fact of the resurrection is enough of a challenge to get him busy preparing for the eternal Reign of God. However, the Gospel writers remind us that Jesus "came preaching" and that Jesus's life and preaching were models of inclusion and redemption that had dramatic impact on people's everyday lives.

The prophetic Christian rejoices in the crucifixion, the resurrection, and the promise of "a home on high" that these events signal. Jesus cried with a loud voice from the cross and promised a thief—a deviant and an outsider—that after their shared suffering would come shared peace and rest in Paradise, which Luke 16:22

calls "Abraham's bosom." However, Jesus also reminds us that the resurrection is meaningless if we do not address the sufferings of those who are "laid at our gate." Jesus's apocalypses (Matthew 24 and 25; Mark 13; Luke 16) are all tied to our behavior toward one another; his images of justice and inclusion are most specifically elaborated in Matthew and Luke.

The enslaved African Americans who used their songs to flag this story of the rich man and Lazarus were a suffering people. They worked in a society that intended for them to remain a permanent servant class of household domestics and farm laborers. As African Americans developed their Christianity, they adopted a very negative perspective on the religion of their masters. Enslaved women and men would have been appalled at the hubris of the rich man in asking Abraham to "send Lazarus" to bring water and to "send him to my father's house." The man is in torment and he is still giving orders!

The response to the rich man who wants his brothers to know what they should do is simply "If they hear not Moses and the prophets, neither will they be persuaded though one rose from the dead." The resurrection is the most elemental and fundamental component in the Christian's confession of faith. Repeatedly we preach and teach that belief in the resurrection is the starting point of our faith. However, this story that Jesus tells, a story remembered by the communities formed in response to Jesus's resurrection, makes meaning of the resurrection contingent upon relations of equity and justice in everyday life. The resurrection is meaningless if we do not live out the commands of the prophets: "do justice, love mercy, and walk humbly with thy God." We have a choice: "Treat Lazarus right!" or expect to face the fire.

Reading the Rich Man and Lazarus

The story of the Rich Man and Lazarus, as Luke 16:19-31 is usually called, has caught the imagination of African Americans and figures in their preaching and music traditions. In addition to numerous sermons about this selfish and arrogant rich man, two spirituals focus on this text: "Rocka My Soul in the Bosom of Abraham" and "I Got a Home in-a That Rock."[10] How do the imaginations of the enslaved women and men who sang about "Po' Lazarus" help Christians today? Enslaved women and men possessed a prophetic-apocalyptic reading of the Bible that envisioned final justice in this world and the next. On its face, the story about the rich man and Lazarus is simply about justice in the other world. Luke depicts the rewards for Lazarus in the next life above, but in sight of, the torments for the rich man. However, the importance that African Americans placed on justice in *this* world is an invitation to explore more deeply the meaning and importance of the story. Since these songs place the rich man and Lazarus within the slave community's canon, it is reasonable to presume that this continued emphasis invites contemporary Christians to hear it, too.

Faithful "Friends of the Mammon of Unrighteousness"

In spite of problems associated with the King James Version of the Bible, including its archaic and androcentric language and the limited manuscript traditions on which the translation is based, I will focus primarily on the King James Version of the story and its surrounding texts. The phrase "bosom of Abraham" appears only in Luke 16:22 and only in the King James Version of the Bible.[11] That the spiritual's reference is to this passage is unequivocal. Recent scholarly translations of the Bible have inserted topic headings into the Gospels that did not exist in the Bible available to literate slaves and to others who facilitated the assimilation of the Bible into African-American oral tradition. Thus, although contemporary translations may guide our eyes to see the story of the rich man and Lazarus within the limits of Luke 16:19-31, to appreciate fully the power of the African-American reading of this text, we should begin our reading with verse 14 or even with Luke 16:1. Chapter 16 begins with a story that contemporary translations term "The Parable of the Dishonest Manager" (vv. 1-13). In that story, Jesus calls the products and profits of the rich "dishonest wealth" (NRSV) or "mammon of unrighteousness" (KJV).

Verses 14-18 comprise the unit "The Law and the Kingdom of God." Here Jesus converses with "the Pharisees also, who were covetous . . ." (KJV), "who were lovers of money" (NRSV). While the translators punctuate the text in a way that implies that loving money was an essential characteristic of all Pharisees, it is more appropriate to see Jesus as conversing with particular Pharisees who were "covetous" or "lovers of money." The concerns and admonitions Jesus expresses point to the distance between love of money and love of God; several hints appear about the negative consequences of the love of money in human relations. After the Pharisees ridicule Jesus ("and they derided him"), Jesus accuses them of putting up a front ("ye . . . justify yourselves" KJV). Jesus then asserts that "that which is highly esteemed among men"—in other words, money—"is abomination in the sight of God" (KJV v. 15b). Jesus warns these lovers of money that their value system is not of God, despite the fact that as Pharisees, they see themselves as the most significant representatives of God and the law. Jesus then reminds them that "the law and the prophets were in effect until John came: since then the good news of the kingdom of God is proclaimed" (NRSV), and everyone "presseth into it" (v. 16 KJV). The good news that Jesus preaches is a continuation of the law *and the prophets.*

Throughout Luke's gospel, the emphasis on "everyone" places "the poor" in the foreground.[12] It is Luke's gospel that informs us of the poverty of Jesus' family (Luke 2:22-24). When Jesus speaks of "everyone," he is talking about those who, whatever the reasons for their poverty, have been excluded from the religious mainstream. These people are unable to offer the material sacrifices necessary for ritual atonement and reconciliation. As many scholars have pointed out, Luke's Gospel mentions a variety of people restricted from participation in Temple ritual and, according to rigid pharisaic notions, from aspects of community life as well.[13] Jesus "show[s] concern for the poor, the infirm, the women, and the pagans" and "takes a clear stand against riches and criticizes the rich."[14]

Jesus invoked "the law and the prophets" to emphasize the central themes of his ministry (Luke 4:18-19), when he declared himself "anointed" to preach "good news to the poor, . . . the captives, . . . the blind, [and] . . . the oppressed." These poor included those excluded from the temple's ritual life. When John's disciples came to inquire "Are you the one who is to come, or are we to wait for another?" Jesus sent them back, saying: "Go your way, and tell John what things ye have seen and heard; how that the blind see, the lame walk, the lepers are cleansed, the deaf hear, the dead are raised, *to the poor the gospel is preached*" (emphasis mine).

The importance and prominence of women in the gospel of Luke may illuminate the passage on divorce at the end of "The Law and the Kingdom of God" (vv. 14-18). Women, especially sinful women like the woman with the alabaster box who anointed Jesus (7:36-50), were included in "the poor." Luke implies that Jesus' affirmation of the woman who anointed him leads to a multitude of women "who had been healed" becoming his disciples and "minister[ing] out of their substance" (8:3). After reminding his listeners that heaven and earth would pass away before one letter in the law, Jesus admonishes: "Whosoever putteth away his wife and marrieth another, committeth adultery: and whosoever marrieth her that is put away from her husband committeth adultery" (16:18).

When Jesus's option for the poor is placed in the foreground, this seeming insertion makes sense. In biblical times, divorced women had very few options. They could go back to their parents' home, if their parents were still living. More often they were forced to appeal for justice to the elders who sat in the gates and who engaged in decision-making for the community. In such circumstances, women became "beggars" at the gates. In spite of its male characters, some of Jesus's hearers may have heard the parable as: (1) an exposition reinforcing this admonition against divorce, and (2) placing divorce in the category of injustice articulated by "the prophets," who were inseparably tied to Jesus' view of the law. The admonition against divorce can be read as an order against creating a situation of structural deprivation, the kind of structural deprivation that victimized "the widows and the orphans"—two of the more visible categories of "the poor" and those excluded from the sacred mainstream.[15] Throughout Luke-Acts, Luke "speaks of widows more than any other New Testament writer."[16]

The Beggars Laid at the Rich Man's Gate

Although the parable of "poor man Lazarus, poor as I," begins with a male beggar laid at a rich man's gate, that beggar could be anyone in the excluded categories about whom Jesus expresses concern. The story itself stands as a challenge to all who are, or wish to be, rich. What happens when people are confronted with a human need and possess the power to help?—They become the targets of divine judgment.

The power of the rich man is emphasized by his "gate." While the text does not place this rich man in the city gates with the elders—a place of power and decision-making—the rich man's gated household does imply a position of power and prominence.

The rich man has the agency, the ability to do something about Lazarus's desperate situation.

Lazarus is laid at the rich man's gate without any explanation of how he became a beggar. Earlier in Luke's gospel and in the other gospels, people pressing into the kingdom—the poor to whom the gospel was preached—were often found begging by the roadside. They were displaced and disinherited, disconnected from society's secure places, whether because of their leprosy, their demons, their blindness, or their lameness. In some cases, the causes of their predicaments, such as demons and unclean spirits, are mentioned. These presumed causes often teach us about the logic of biblical times, which sought explanations for personal troubles in a troubled relationship with God. In John 9, for instance, people ask "Who sinned?" that a man was born blind.

In Luke 16, Jesus does not explain the cause of Lazarus's troubles; he simply presents Lazarus at the rich man's gate and tells us that the rich man had the power to make a difference but did not. One sermon I heard on this text, "Treat Lazarus Right," emphasized the importance of our *not* knowing why Lazarus was poor and who laid him at the gate. The preacher stopped in the middle of the sermon and appealed to God to bless the dogs who did at least lick Lazarus's sores. In contrast, one might imagine that the Pharisees, listening to this parable, might have viewed the dogs and their connection with Lazarus as a magnification of Lazarus's uncleanness and a justification for separating him from the clean and well-to-do. In Jesus's telling, however, Lazarus's intrinsic moral worth is dramatically underscored.

Dogs were the garbage workers of biblical society. They consumed "the crumbs" from the rich man's table. Those crumbs were edible and substantial, because pieces of bread ("the crumbs") functioned as napkins for wealthy diners. They wiped their hands with the bread and then tossed it under the table to the dogs. Lazarus, the human about whom God cares, was treated worse than these unclean dogs.[17]

The common humanity of both men comes through clearly. Both hunger. One hopes to eat the crumbs from the rich man's table, while the other dines sumptuously. Both die. One has no earthly helper and must be carried to Abraham's bosom by the angels, while the other has friends and family to carry him to his grave, where he is buried. Both find themselves in an afterlife that places them before the sight of God ("the bosom of Abraham") at the same time, one to dwell in eternal comfort and the other in eternal torment.

The rich man is clueless about God's concern for the beggar and his own obligations as a rich man. He looks up and sees Lazarus in Abraham's bosom. Not realizing that the logic of the world he has known has been turned upside down, the rich man calls out from Hell to "Father Abraham": "have pity on me and send Lazarus to dip the tip of his finger in water and cool my tongue, because I am in agony in this fire" (v. 24). Suddenly the rich man needs Lazarus and calls him by name. However, he requests that Father Abraham *send* Lazarus to provide cooling water—the rich man remains so arrogant that he assumes Lazarus should serve him in the afterlife.

This is precisely the kind of arrogance and presumptuousness of the wealthy that Jesus spoke against frequently in his ministry. In Matt. 19:23, Jesus taught, "a rich man shall hardly enter into the kingdom of heaven" (KJV). Jesus reminded his disciples (and by extension, us) that greatness is tied to our willingness to be servants and not to be served (Matt. 20:20-28). Yet the rich man was still seeking to be served! Jesus told his disciples, "Indeed there are last who shall be first, and there are first who shall be last" (Luke 13:30 KJV). In the parable of the wedding banquet (Matt. 22:1-14), Jesus described God's response to the arrogance of rich people with his story of the king who invites the good and bad to be his guests instead of his wealthy peers. Jesus wanted his listeners to understand that their refusal to see and hear poor people in this world absolutely contradicted God's will.

Abraham let the rich man know that it was now time for Lazarus to be comforted: "But Abraham said, Son, remember that thou in thy lifetime receivedst thy good things, and likewise Lazarus evil things: but now he is comforted, and thou art tormented. And beside all this, between us and you there is a great gulf fixed: so that they which would pass from hence to you cannot; neither can they pass to us, that would come from thence" (vv. 25-26 KJV).

Following Abraham's explanation, the rich man wanted to send someone to his brothers to "warn them" and to prevent their ending up in "this place of torment." Abraham stressed the importance of not only the law but the prophets: "They have Moses and the prophets; let them hear them" (v. 29).

The conclusion of Jesus's parable speaks volumes to us about the importance of taking seriously the plight of those who are poor and otherwise excluded from the "good things." The rich man believed this message would be more powerful for his brothers when it came from someone who returned from the dead. Remember, Jesus is speaking to the Pharisees—religious leaders defined by their belief in resurrection. The resurrection, Paul teaches, is at the heart of the good news and has created the opening to bring in the Gentiles (Romans 6:3-9). In spite of the tremendous miracle of someone returning from the dead, Luke's gospel forces us to hear Jesus's voice say, "If they hear not Moses and the prophets, neither will they be persuaded, though one rose from the dead."

Christians are reminded that we cannot "omit the weightier matters of the law, judgment, mercy, and faith" (Matt 23:23 KJV). Confronted with what matters to God—the plight of those who are sick, hungry, thirsty, homeless, imprisoned, and oppressed— we are charged to respond. These are the weighty matters of the law that the prophets emphasize over and over again as the Spirit moves them to remind ancient Israel of its covenant with God. Jesus is telling us that "the law and the prophets" are at the foundation of the gospel; those of us who hear Jesus are required to hear "the law *and the prophets*" as well.

Jesus is describing authentic faith. One cannot believe in Jesus as the Savior of the world if one does not believe in and practice the justice, mercy, and love received by "the prophets." The Gospels are popularly characterized as lengthy introductions to the crucifixion and resurrection; Christian baptismal and confirmation confessions include statements of belief in the resurrection of Jesus the Christ. Jesus, however, points out that the resurrection is meaningless without hearing "Moses and the prophets."

Many observers of African-American religious experience have noted the prominence of the Old Testament in songs, prayers, stories, and sermons. These are so prominent that sometimes people ignore the tremendous emphasis on the crucifixion and resurrection within this same body of African-American songs, prayers, stories, and sermons. Songs about the rich man and Lazarus emphasize a biblical text that invites hearers to hear Moses and the prophets. For nineteenth-century listeners and singers, the God who parted the Red Sea for Moses is the same God who was proclaimed by Jesus. As followers of Jesus, they were tied to God's initial act of liberation and to a continuing divine concern for human liberation as carried forward by "the prophets." For those who ignore the call to participate in this divine liberation, the resurrection loses its *redemptive* power and becomes a meaningless event. Jesus' call to disciples, as followers and students, as Christians, is to engage the beggars laid at their gates— to do justice, love mercy, and walk humbly (Micah 6:8).

Making the Resurrection Matter in an Age of Prosperity

Christians in the United States are bombarded with all sorts of messages about affluence and prosperity. This is particularly true in many of the religious programs presented on television: some televangelists, themselves formerly poor, insist, almost to the exclusion of other topics, that believers' tithing and offering practices are directly related to their abilities to earn, save money, and enjoy the kind of life that constitutes the American dream. While these televangelists are quick to insist that we are "no longer under the law" and should not be legalistic in approaching the Christian faith, they fail to mention the "weightier matters of the law," which Jesus insisted were paramount. As a result, Christians in this rich country, both those who are wealthy and those who want to be, do not "hear Moses and the prophets."

This failure to hear Moses and the prophets is of particular concern to evangelical Christians who, like Jim Wallis, the editor of *Sojourners* magazine, hold "a progressive and prophetic vision of faith and politics."[18] The 2004 presidential and congressional elections in the United States spotlighted conservative evangelical Christians. Denominational bodies, televangelists, and faith-based organizations rallied around the issues of abortion ("pro-life agenda") and same-sex marriage ("defense of marriage and the family"). Jim Wallis characterized the aftermath of the election as "one of those where, no matter who won, almost half the population was going to feel absolutely crushed."[19] We are now deeply divided, the media say, between "red states" (Republican) and "blue states" (Democrat).[20] Wallis points out that

> [a] very smart group of Republican strategists effectively appealed to both the faith and the fears of an important conservative religious constituency.

> The religious Right fought to keep the primary focus on gay marriage and abortion (two important issues) and

some of their leaders even said that good Christians could only vote for George Bush.[21]

In the world's most affluent and powerful nation, wealth, power, and the relationship between the poor and the affluent are significant factors in social policy and political conflict. On one hand, the conservative approach to poverty has been to emphasize individual and personal responsibility and the ways that the immoral choices made by people who are poor have contributed to their misery. On the other hand, liberal approaches have emphasized the structural conditions and historical forces that create poverty, as well as the personal and social disorganization associated with poverty.

Biblical prophets often illuminated the ways in which people were made poor. Amos pointed to the complicity of the rich in the immiseration of others. The Torah called for a safety net for the poor (for example, leave enough grain in the field for the poor and the stranger to "glean" [Lev. 19:10]) and periodic corrections to the accumulation of wealth (the jubilee [Lev. 25:8-17]). Tithing—the payment of one's obligations to God—included the payment of one's obligations to the poor. Overall, the weight of the Hebrew biblical witness stood against political and economic oppression and stood for aiding brothers (and sisters) who were or became poor. The memory lessons included in the Torah admonished the people of God to remember when they were oppressed so that they would not "oppress" the "stranger" (for example, Deut. 24:14-18).

The story of the rich man and Lazarus is a warning to all who are rich or want to be rich. Today, wealth or its appearance is celebrated in popular literature not only in pictures of celebrities and their "bling" but also in prices and shopping information about their clothes and accessories. Too often, rich Christians fail to attend to the needs of the poor and to hear Moses and the prophets. If such wealthy Christians do not wish to celebrate the resurrection of Jesus "unworthily" (KJV) or "in an unworthy manner" (1 Cor. 11:27), then they must hear Moses and the prophets and heed the call to attend to people who are poor and excluded.

Christians in the United States face not only the inequities of race, ethnicity, sexual orientation, gender, and physical abilities but poverty, which leaves thousands of people dying daily of HIV/AIDS and other preventable illnesses. These people are laid at the gates of a nation where many have defined morality as a political issue. If we hear Moses and the prophets, then we know that our relationship with those who are poor, hungry, naked, bound, and sick (Matt. 25:31-46) will be interrogated. If we cannot give an account that places us on the right hand of the King, then it will not matter that Jesus was crucified and rose from the dead. The response of rich Christians to the beggars laid at their gates will determine whether or not the resurrection really matters to them. In order for Jesus' death and resurrection to matter, we must "hear Moses and the prophets" and respond accordingly.

Study Questions

1. How do the images of African-American experience described in this essay connect with your experience? What surprises you? What excites or encourages you? What troubles you?

2. What similarities and dissimilarities does Gilkes find between Poor Man Lazarus and African Americans? How do you understand these comparisons? Where do you see yourself in these comparisons?

3. What are the roles of Poor Man Lazarus in the relation to the rich man? How does their relation play out in terms of classism in the United States? Reflecting this analysis, how do racism and classism play in the African-American context?

4. How do you identify the African-American prophetic tradition in the story of the Poor Man Lazarus? What are the prophetic traditions that could bring justice in this world? What prophetic voices are speaking around you? What prophetic words are you invited to speak?

5. How does this African-American biblical reading change your interpretation of the Bible? How do you feel about this change?

II. A Postcolonial Reading

Sexual Morality and National Politics

Reading Biblical "Loose Women"
Kwok Pui-lan

Perspective

In 1995, I published *Discovering the Bible in the Non-Biblical World*, one of the first books to discuss biblical interpretation in the social, religious, and cultural contexts of Asia. After the book was published, I received interesting reviews from scholars in biblical studies, Asian theology, and mission studies. Some hailed the book as groundbreaking because it calls for a radical reorientation of biblical studies to take into consideration religious pluralism and issues of class, gender, race, and culture.[1] Others expressed caution because they thought my approach downplays biblical authority, my interpretation favors a particular audience, and my ideological stance shapes it.[2] These contrasting responses clearly show that biblical scholars and theologians have divergent views of what the Bible is, what counts as revelation, and what is involved in the interpretive process.

Some might think this essay is pointedly political, for I will comment on the use of religious rhetoric, fueled by certain interpretations of the Bible, during the 2004 presidential election in the United States of America. But I want to emphasize that the choice to remain silent about the current political situation is a political decision itself and should not be presumed to be value-free or neutral. To honor the Rev. Dr. Anna Howard Shaw, a Methodist pioneer (1847-1919) who spoke out courageously on such social issues as temperance, women's suffrage, and peace during her lifetime, I shall discuss the relationship between sexual morality and national politics, knowing fully that it is a highly contentious subject. Precisely because it is so controversial, theological communities, including teachers, students, pastors, and lay leaders, need to debate these issues and to learn from each other.

The Christian community does not have a monolithic understanding or consensus about how the Bible should be interpreted. On one hand, there are Christians who think, as I do, that the Bible emerged from the history and cultures of the Hebrew people and early Christian communities and must be read against that backdrop. Each generation of Christians brings new questions, as well as its own insights, in comprehending God's continuous revelation in history to the text. For example, in *Navigating Romans through Cultures*, scholars from Africa, Latin America, Asia, Europe, and North America seek to express Paul's understanding of the Gospel in their own contexts.[3]

On the other hand, a significant number of Christians in America believe the Bible is the literal Word of God. Because few readers know the Bible's original languages, God's revelation is gleaned through literal reading of the biblical text in English translation. These readers insist that being a Christian means abiding by the timeless moral precepts and religious teachings inscribed in the Bible as taught by the pastors and religious leaders of their churches. In the opinion of these Christians, others who take a more liberal view of scriptural interpretation are not faithful to the biblical witness. Moreover, they often blame liberal Christians for causing moral confusion and decay, for the gradual erosion of family values, and for other social ills and discontent.

The 2004 U.S. presidential election demonstrated conclusively that biblical interpretation has very high stakes in American national politics. Shortly after the election, people circulated imaginative cartographical depictions of the post-election United States over the Internet. One map depicted the more liberal blue states joining their northern neighbor to become the United States of Canada, while the red states formed a new coalition called Jesusland.[4] There is a certain sarcasm in labeling the American inland *Jesusland*. As portrayed by the liberal media, this part of the country is populated by people with conservative Christian values who voted for President George W. Bush and who politically lean toward the right. Christian leaders in Jesusland are presumed to be dogmatic in their religious worldview, conservative in their social agenda, and overconfident in prescribing moral values for everybody.

The Relevance of Postcolonial Criticism

As a formerly colonized person born in the British colony of Hong Kong, I have always been curious about the intersection of faith and politics. When the Western colonial empires invaded other peoples' lands and colonized vast numbers of peoples, what were the Christians—including their theologians and leaders—thinking and doing? I want to make some connection between colonization in the nineteenth century and the rising American imperialism we are witnessing today.

During the heyday of colonialism, European powers and the United States justified occupying other peoples' lands by claiming it was for the natives' own good, since they would be able to hear the Gospel and benefit from education, health care, and other Western cultural products. Spreading the Gospel was an integral part of the civilizing mission and was assumed to be part of "the white man's burden." *How England Saved China*, published in the 1910s by a British writer, captured the sentiment at the time.[5]

Given today's understanding of the separation between church and state, it may not be politically savvy for American politicians to declare that the Christian West has the burden of saving the Muslim Middle East. Although overt Christian rhetoric has been replaced by secular language, however, the same missionary zeal is evident in the current political rhetoric of bringing democracy to other peoples in the world. Under the veneer of a self-proclaimed mission of spreading "freedom" and "democracy" lurks the self-congratulatory assurance that Christian culture is more developed and civilized than other cultures. Behind the secular rhetoric lies the arrogance of political messianism fueled by certain understandings of God, the Bible, and Christian responsibility in the world. After all, it is no secret that George W. Bush is a born-again Christian who frequently talks about his own faith, employs biblical rhetoric, and imagines the world as the site of an apocalyptic struggle between good and evil.

Before the final debate between the 2004 U.S. presidential candidates, Boston journalist David Nyhan said that the debate would be about God, guns, and gays. This succinct statement captures the essence of the 2004 presidential election: the focus on faith, the war on terrorism, and moral values. While the media expected the war against terrorism to feature prominently in political campaigns after September 11, 2001, many commentators were taken by surprise when exit polls showed that "moral values" was the issue that mattered most to the largest number of voters, surpassing terrorism and the economy. Soon after the election, some commentators argued that the Democrats had lost the election over the issue of gay marriage. Political analysts have discussed in great detail how the ballot question of a state constitutional amendment banning gay marriage propelled people to vote out of fear that the nation had lost its moral compass. According to the *Boston Globe*, the group Citizens for Community Values not only worked to put the issue of a constitutional amendment banning gay marriage on the Ohio ballot but also inserted 2.5 million pamphlets into church bulletins the Sunday before the general election and made 850,000 phone calls before the polls opened, reminding people to vote.[6]

Because sexual morality and national politics are currently so intertwined in the United States, with significant implications for the whole world, biblical scholars and theologians must assume the responsibility of searching for critical insights to illuminate the situation. Discourses about the Bible must always be seen in the wider contexts of cultural and religious ethos, as well as of changing economic and political configurations. I have stated that biblical interpretation is about the "politics of truth."[7] In today's America, biblical interpretation is not just a religious discourse for and among Christians; it is also a public and political discourse shaping the values and decision making of the nation.

Postcolonial studies have special relevance for analyzing the current political situation, the so-called culture war, and the heated debates about gay marriage. Emerging in the 1970s, postcolonial studies have exerted decisive influence in the fields of humanities and social sciences. Postcolonial scholars have developed strategies and tactics to dislodge us from the colonial syndrome, debunk Eurocentric assumptions in knowledge building and theorizing, use a global perspective to unmask white hegemony, and interpret literary texts and cultural phenomena from the viewpoints of people who are colonized, exiled, diasporized, and marginalized. The authors of *The Empire Writes Back* argue:

More than any other concept, the postcolonial has facilitated the gradual disturbance of the Eurocentric dominance of academic debate, and has empowered postcolonial intellectuals to redirect discussion towards issues of direct political relevance to the non-Western world.[8]

Postcolonial analysis highlights the integral relationship between political and military dimensions of empire building and their religious justifications and cultural configurations. At a time when the United States has become the sole current superpower waging a global war against terrorism, alienating many of its allies as well as the people in the global South, the use of postcolonial theory will prove very timely. We can see in sharp relief why the war in Iraq can be linked to discussions about sexual morality and the suppression of gays and lesbians at home. Joe Lockard has insightfully observed:

Morality under the Bush administration is not morality in the sense of social fair play; rather, invoking morality has become a politicized mode of illegitimate desire-fulfillment, an expression of Christian evangelical lust for possession of the American body politic.[9]

The war in Iraq is an integral part of the U.S. strategy for exerting global dominance. In his timely book *The New Imperialism*, David Harvey details the significance of control over the Middle East for American economic and political domination, especially in its competition for hegemony with the European Union and China. With in-depth analysis, Harvey points out that whoever controls the oil supply of the Middle East will dictate global economic growth for the next fifty years.[10] In a similar vein, Noam Chomsky describes how the war in Iraq is part of an "imperial grand strategy" devised for "the most powerful state in history to maintain its hegemony through the threat or the use of military force, the dimension of power in which it reigns supreme."[11] Such a grand strategy cannot succeed at home and abroad without a massive cultural and media campaign to manufacture consensus and to influence public opinion.

Given the enormous influence of Christianity in America, churches and religious organizations must be enlisted to provide religious blessing and legitimation in this aggressive march to global dominance. Faith and patriotism are subliminally joined when the words "God bless America" are proclaimed. As William Countryman notes:

> Public figures will appeal to Protestant values, not by cit-
> ing the distinctive beliefs of particular churches . . ., but
> by appealing to the Bible, regarded by Protestantism as
> the fountainhead of religion. Protestantism is, in effect,
> the culture religion of the United States.[12]

Countryman observes that religious discourse in the United States always tends to circle around discourse about the Bible.[13] The Bible is cited by religious leaders and public pundits to oppose same-sex marriage and to reinforce women's subordination, their second-class status in the public arena, and capitalist economy. It is no coincidence that the two hot button moral issues for the Christian Right are abortion and homosexuality, for the control of women's bodies and the policing of sexuality go hand in hand with compulsory heterosexuality.

The Political Climate of Biblical Interpretation in the United States

In the past twenty-five years, public discourse on faith and religion in the United States has turned increasingly conservative. Conservative foundations have funded think tanks to point American religion in conservative directions. In 2003 alone, over $7,000,000 was channeled to such think tanks—for example, the Institute for Religion and Democracy and the Institute on Religion and Public Life. These think tanks have developed strategies to influence public opinion and social policy and created right-wing advocacy groups within mainline churches. Under the guise of "family values," they seek to attack affirmative action, equality between the sexes, reproductive rights, and justice for lesbians and gays.[14] Partly as a result of their work, mainline churches have become embroiled in bitter and divisive debates about gay and lesbian issues; and this emotion-laden discussion is playing out in a much larger political arena as well.

It is sometimes difficult to imagine what kind of message those members of mainline church circles are getting about the

Bible and sexual morality. In her study of the story of Sodom and Gomorrah (Gen 19:1-29) on the Internet, Susanne Scholz has pointed to the vast amount of materials on the Bible, including thousands of web pages on this story alone.[15] Both individuals and organizations publicize their viewpoints in these discussions of the Bible. The volume of web pages using Sodom and Gomorrah to condemn homosexuality is immense, and the language is especially acrimonious. Scholz notes that academic discussions of the Bible rarely surface in the digital media, which means that the kinds of exegesis and interpretations we are learning at seminaries rarely reach the public. Internet discussions of the Bible are part of contemporary digital culture, yet progressive scholars and religious leaders pay insufficient attention to them. Writing on the Bible and the digital media, Robert S. Fortner notes that the digital media are constructing a new culture—a virtual reality, if you will—that will "reconfigure the symbolic world of humankind and the methodology for recognizing truth."[16] Progressive Christians will lose ground if we fail to use the digital media to compete in the marketplace of ideas and public opinion.

Given this analysis of our national political situation and the culture, what are the implications for progressive Christians and for study of the Bible?

First, it is insufficient to ask, "What does the Bible say?" without asking the corollary question, "How is the Bible used today?" Asking "What does the Bible say?" not only creates the impression that the meaning of the Bible is self-evident but also camouflages the power issue behind the claim—that is, "Who says so and why?" This question requires us to pay attention to the religious rhetoric used in biblical texts and to the redeployment of such rhetoric to serve today's political purposes. As a matter of fact, biblical scholars have increasingly paid attention to the rhetorical character of biblical discourse, seeing biblical texts not as windows to reality but as language used in particular social and political situations to persuade, to present an argument, to form opinion, and to motivate people to action.[17] When Paul commanded in 1 Cor. 14:34 that "women should be silent in the churches," he was directing his argument to a particular church context and using rhetoric to establish his authority, form opinion, and shape behavior. He was not treating women as his equals when he demanded silence, subordination, and obedience.[18] When Paul's authority is appealed to today and his rhetoric is repeated, it is being used to influence public opinion and to shape particular behavior in churches and in the larger society.

Second, progressive Christians must begin strategizing how to educate the Christian community, as well as the public, on the Bible's teachings on sexuality. Kathleen M. Sands has pointed out:

> The particular inaudibility of progressive religion on issues of sexuality and reproduction has a tremendous cost now, when these have become at once the site of religion's greatest authority and the ideological centerpiece of politics.[19]

While the Christian Right has devised a clear strategy and spoken in unequivocal terms, mainline churches have captured media attention only when the question of sexuality has threatened to divide the church or to cause scandals, such as clergy sex abuse, ordination of gay men and lesbians, and in-church blessing of same-sex couples. The media have become obsessed with church scandals and the issue of homosexuality, yet have provided few opportunities for substantial debates and education of the public. People outside the church may not know the finer points of theological arguments and the amount of biblical evidence marshaled in church synods, ecclesiastical courts, and conventions. All they know is that mainline denominations are a house divided, and it is almost impossible to obtain clear guidance on anything related to sexuality or morality. It is important that mainline churches work together to educate the American public about critical approaches to the Bible as a key component in the overall strategy to effect social and cultural changes. Instead of treating sex as a taboo subject or focusing only on issues pertaining to homosexuality, Christian churches need to foster a healthy, holistic understanding of human sexuality based on a liberating and justice-seeking reading of the Bible.

Third, progressive Christians are ill advised to maintain a dichotomous view of personal and social morality. After the 2004 election, I heard commentators say that the Christian Right focuses on personal morality but neglects social concerns, such as poverty, that are moral issues also. There is some truth to this assertion. Jim Wallis repeatedly points out in public interviews that the three thousand biblical verses about the poor greatly outnumber the verses on the sexuality of same-sex couples.[20] But the feminist movement has long taught us that the personal is political, and the late French philosopher Michel Foucault insisted that sexuality must be interpreted within the societal structures and networks of power, of domination and suppression.[21] The Christian Right has clearly grasped the political nature of the debate on human sexuality; George W. Bush was able to claim that he had gained "political capital" in the months immediately following his 2004 election.

This last point has significant implications for reading biblical passages pertaining to sex, gender, and morality. We need to pass beyond the stage of finding proof texts from the Bible to support one view or the other on controversial sexual or moral issues. Instead, we need to see that sexuality is always embedded and inscribed in larger societal structures and political discourses. Postcolonial critics such as Homi Bhabha and the late Edward Said have insisted that "the home" and "the world" are mutually constituted and constantly affect one another. For example, Said clearly argued that what is happening in the English home in Jane Austen's novel, *Mansfield Park*, cannot be separated from the imperial reach of the empire in the plantations in Antigua.[22] Similarly, Toni Morrison uses what happens at home in her novel, *Beloved*, to illuminate the American institutions of racism and slavery.[23]

Using such a critical postcolonial perspective, I shall explore how racial minority female theologians and biblical scholars have contributed to our understanding of the intersection between gender, sexuality, and national politics. Specifically, I want to focus on the ways gender and sexuality intertwine with race/ethnicity, class, culture, religion, and power in the Bible and in biblical interpretation. These scholars have presented models of reading the Bible that do not limit gender and sexuality to the private realm or frame the discussion primarily in terms of the inequality of the two sexes. Instead, they offer an interactive and multifaceted reading that has much to do with the history and cultural politics of American society. Collectively, they have examined racial/ethnic dynamics, sexual violence against women, and the blaming of women for evils in society in biblical texts, contributing to a growing body of critical interpretations by racial minority women and women in the Third World.

Sampling Interpretation

From a postcolonial perspective, I want to highlight the significance of the womanist discourse in shaping new awareness of the national history of the United States. I will first consider the contribution of womanist interpretations of the story of Hagar in the book of Genesis. In her pioneering study, Delores S. Williams uses the story of Hagar as a key to illumine the situation of African-American women and the contours of their social and cultural experience as shaped by the institution of slavery.[24] Her method of biblical interpretation, her challenge of the liberationist paradigm, her understanding of the motifs of survival and quality of life, her use of new resources such as literature and music for theology, and her critique of surrogacy and traditional atonement theories have engendered a rich and fascinating womanist discourse.[25]

In focusing on Hagar, Williams and her womanist colleagues revisit one of the foundational stories of the Hebrew Bible—God's covenant with Abraham and the myth of the chosen people. Williams's work offers a counternarrative to the traditional interpretation, which emphasizes God's promise to Abraham, Isaac, Jacob, and their descendents to make them a strong nation. She challenges us to see that at a critical moment in the formation of a people, this slave girl, her child, and others were marginalized and excluded. Just as postcolonial critics challenge the formation of national myths and the narration of nationhood,[26] so Williams demands that we enlarge our historical imagination to include the foreigner, the enslaved, the surrogate, and the domestic maid— social contemporaries of the "patriarchs" or "matriarchs" whom we cherish and choose to remember. Constructing a counter-memory, Renee K. Harrison laments that the formation of Israel as a people, and later as a nation, has a steep price, for Hagar must submit to oppression and "endure the trauma of rape, bare a son, and fulfill a role of coerced surrogacy for the purpose of *future* nation building" (emphasis Harrison's).[27]

The womanist discourse on the Hagar story has important implications for understanding American history and its foundational myths. In *Chosen People*, journalist Clifford Longley writes that the English, and later the Americans, viewed their situation as analogous to that of the ancient Israelites: just as God selected the Jews in the past, God has chosen them and for the same purpose. They have a special destiny in human history.[28] The womanist theologians challenge such an assumed overlapping of the biblical story and the history of American people for two reasons. On one hand, they insist we cannot simply remember God's covenant with Abraham while forgetting the slavery, sexual violence, and coerced surrogacy epitomized by the story of Hagar. On the other hand, they point to the institution of slavery, in which enslaved women were systemically abused and sexually violated, as an inseparable component of the formation of the American state.

Williams also calls attention to the disturbing relationship between Hagar and Sarah caused by their unequal positions in the family and society. Sarah's sexuality is blessed, and her child Isaac can inherit his father's promise. The slave girl's sexuality is viewed with jealousy and suspicion, and her child is cast out into the wilderness. In her critique of white women's privileges and their narrow focus on patriarchy, Williams argues that white women and black women are constructed differently as national subjects. The state apparatus and the white institutions offer protection and privileges to white women, but black women are discriminated against in what she labels persistent "colorism" in society.[29] Williams and her womanist colleagues challenge any claims of America's manifest destiny, as well as that unchecked arrogance with which America insists that it is called to bring freedom to the world in the current political messianism. Such claims are ironic when America has yet to deal honestly with the hypocrisy of its national myths, which constantly seek to repress the truths of slavery and sexual violation of black women.

Gale A. Yee, a Chinese-American biblical scholar who specializes in the Hebrew Bible, offers another model of reading that sheds light on contemporary American politics. Using the method of ideological criticism, Yee investigates the use of women as the symbolic incarnation of moral evil, sin, carnality, and destruction in the Hebrew Bible. A critical scrutiny of the connection between women and evil is necessary, Yee explains, because "[a]s a foundational text in Western civilization, the Bible has been and continues to be a significant *fons et origo* of religious and social attitudes about gender, race/ethnicity, class, and colonialism."[30] Her research also is prompted by her social location as an Asian-American biblical scholar who lives in a culture in which popular media often portray Asian women using Orientalist stereotypes—for example, the Dragon Lady, Suzy Wong, the Japanese geisha, and the Mongol slave girl.[31]

Utilizing the insights provided by the critics Terry Eagleton and Fredric Jameson, Yee argues that the symbolization and figuration of women as evil and wicked in the Bible must be read against the class struggle and social contradictions of a given time, as well the ideology behind the production of the text. She explains her method as follows: "An ideological criticism presumes . . . that the text is a symbolic resolution of real contradictions, inventing imaginary or formal 'solutions' to unresolved ideological dilemmas."[32] Yee's materialist analysis of the mode of production and the role of governing elites behind the ideological production of texts presents a reading that often jolts readers out of familiar patterns of interpretation and demands that they ask new questions. For example, feminist theologians and biblical scholars have discussed for some time the significance of the story in Genesis 2–3 that has been used to justify women's subordination to men and to symbolize women as sexual and evil. Yee has instead squarely placed the text within the transition from a familial mode of production to a tributary political system, with its more stratified, hierarchical social relations between ruling elites and peasants in an increasingly centralized territorial state during the rise of monarchy. Instead of interpreting the fall in Genesis 3 as symbolizing the inherent corruption of human nature, Gale argues that symbolizing women as evil must be seen in the context of the rupture of gender relationship, one part of the rift between God and humanity, between people and king. Eve's punishment for disobedience and for creating disorder reflects the need to tighten the husband's rule over his wife. A symbolic parallel can be drawn between the people and the king—another prescription ordained and sanctioned by God.[33]

Yee's ideological criticism of the Hebrew Bible provides insights that can be applied to American society and its social and class contradictions today. In postindustrial American society, the forces of globalization have brought new social stress and tension; outsourcing is but one of the more evident examples. The war against terrorism and the need to establish the dominance of American military power have channeled valuable resources away from meeting domestic social needs. The fear and insecurity created in the aftermath of September 11, 2001, have allowed tighter control by the state—for example, the passage of the Patriot Act. The vulnerability of the nation and the desire to protect the *homeland* are used to justify patrolling and sealing the country' borders, waging war against terrorists, and exerting economic and political pressure against those who dare to stand in the way of "American interests." The contradiction produced by rising American imperialism undergirds the ideological production of a discourse that calls for stricter policing of the order, purity, and boundaries of the bourgeois social body—hence the debates on late-term abortion, the sanctity of the marriage institution, and the amendment of state and possibly national constitutions to exclude and limit the rights of gay and lesbian couples.

As we have seen from the foregoing discussion, biblical interpretation has implications not only for American politics but also for the struggle for peace and survival of the world's people. The conservative forces of the American empire will continue to exert pressure and demand readings of the Bible that serve the interests of big multinational corporations and the status quo. Because biblical interpretation has become a site of resistance, biblical critics and theologians must be conscious of the global consequence of our work, foster dialogue, and build coalitions with colleagues in other parts of the world. In the past, the Bible has been strategically deployed to denounce slavery and to promote women's emancipation. Today, it is imperative that it be used to protect women's reproductive rights and the civil rights of gay, lesbian, bisexual, and transgendered people, as well as to resist and challenge American imperialism.

Reading Biblical "Loose Women"

As feminist biblical scholars and theologians, we have recovered and articulated the importance of strong female protagonists in the Bible. Women such as Miriam, Deborah, Mary the mother of Jesus, Prisca, Phoebe, the Syrophoenician woman, and Shiphrah and Puah, the midwives who save Moses' life, have been treated with respect and reclaimed as inspiring role models and foremothers. We have also shed our tears, expressed our sympathy, and vowed never to forget the tragedies of Hagar in the wilderness, the sacrifice of Jephthah's unnamed daughter, the rape of Tamar, and the plights of other biblical women who suffered unspeakable violence.

We can find a place for the heroines and the victims of biblical times in our memories and interpretive frameworks without much difficulty, because they do not challenge our sense of intelligibility as feminists. But what about female figures who somehow fall outside accepted societal norms, whose behaviors challenge social expectations of decency?

In her provocative book *Indecent Theology*, Marcella Althaus-Reid charges that much of the discourse of feminist theology can be considered tame and safe because it revolves around gender and rarely troubles the dangerous waters of sex and sexuality, especially the kinds of sexual expression that irritate middle class, white, vanilla sensibilities.[34] In a pointed way, she also charges that although feminist theologians, including liberationists, have condemned classism and other forms of exploitation, they are often trapped in a binary and dualistic construction of gender and remain oblivious to their own heterosexual biases.[35] Consequently, even as they raise their voices on behalf of the poor and the oppressed, they continue to work within what is defined as decent and acceptable by the heterosexual regime.

I am going to make use of the insights of postcolonial studies here to interpret stories of "loose women" in the Bible—women who are social deviants, licentious and socially unrespectable, and women who exist outside of heterosexual marriage or the protection of a patriarchal family. Although a number of female biblical figures fit this profile, I shall limit my discussion to Rahab the prostitute and to women who exchange "natural intercourse for unnatural" (Rom. 1:26). My goal is not to present an exhaustive study but to highlight salient facets of the postcolonial approach that can be applied to reading the Bible.

Rahab the Harlot: Sinner, Heroine, or Sellout?

The story of Rahab in Joshua 2 is well known. Rahab was a prostitute living in Jericho. When Joshua dispatched two spies to cross the Jordan and reconnoiter the land, they spent the night in her house (Josh. 2:1). The king of Jericho sent out orders to search for the men, but Rahab tricked the king's messengers by hiding the spies on her roof under stalks of flax. She then told the spies that Yahweh, who led the Hebrews out of Egypt and dried up the Red Sea, had promised to give their people the land of Canaan. In return for protecting the spies, Rahab made them promise to spare her family during the siege of Jericho. When the walls surrounding Jericho fell, the Israelites charged inside, ruthlessly killed men and women, young and old, oxen, sheep, and donkeys (6:21), and burned the city. But the prostitute Rahab's family was spared, and "her family has lived in Israel ever since" (6:25).

Rahab is named in Jesus' genealogy at the beginning of Matthew's gospel, together with Tamar, Ruth, and the wife of Uriah

(1:1-18). Since the period of the church fathers, theologians and commentators have attempted to provide plausible reasons for their inclusion in Jesus' genealogy. Jerome was probably the first to suggest that these women shared a common background as sinners; their inclusion highlighted God's grace and Christ's messianic role in saving people from their sins, according to God's promise. Other commentators focused not on the sinful nature of these four women but on their unusual marital or sexually scandalous circumstances.[36] For example, Raymond Brown and others have proposed that these four women appear in response to accusations that Mary's child was illegitimate, conceived out of wedlock. Brown writes, "It is the combination of the scandalous or irregular union and of divine intervention through the woman that explains best Matthew's choice in the genealogy."[37] In contrast, feminist critics use a different interpretive frame and do not indict Rahab as a sinner in order to support a theological claim. Instead, they express sympathy for female figures living on the margins of society.

Before I discuss these feminist interpretations further, I will note that Rahab is not among the biblical women whom feminist biblical scholars have preferred to analyze. Compared with the number of writings on Eve, Sarah and Hagar, Ruth, Esther, and Jephthah's daughter, Rahab the harlot has had fewer interpreters, especially among white feminist scholars. Most feminist commentators have focused on Rahab's role as a prostitute, or her status and reputation, as well as the crucial role she plays in the capture of Jericho. They discuss and elucidate Rahab's marginal status as a "loose" woman living in a brothel or public inn instead of among her kinfolk, pointing out that Rahab lived on the city's periphery, where outcasts and other marginalized groups usually resided. Though some have suggested, based on this story, that harlots were not stigmatized in ancient Israel or in Canaanite society, Phyllis Bird has argued to the contrary: "The harlot is never allowed to become a good wife, but only a good harlot, a righteous outcast, a noble-hearted courtesan, the exception that proves the rule."[38]

A comparison of interpretations by white scholars and postcolonial critics from marginalized communities shows significant differences in their approach and emphasis. White scholars with a feminist bent highlight the role and agency of the female protagonist, even though she is a harlot. Bird, for example, suggests that Rahab is portrayed as a "heroine" in the story because "she protects the Israelite spies, and as a consequence, contributes to Israel's victory." Bird further observes that the biblical editor of this story has fashioned Rahab into "the pagan confessor, the one who discerns what others fail to see, and the one who commits her life to the people of Yahweh. She is wiser than the king of Jericho, and also more clever."[39] Bird's reading reclaims the positive action and speech of the individual female heroine—a common strategy employed by white feminists reading stories of biblical women.

Danna Nolan Fewell and David Gunn suggest that Rahab subverts the patriarchal notion of binary opposites: the outsider becomes the insider; the pagan can quote Deuteronomy with more facility than the Israelites; and the foreigner shows great loyalty and courage. They propose that Rahab can be considered a trickster or a survivor: in the face of extreme odds, a violent god, and a violent people, her religious confession is a way to survive. In the midst of rumors floating around about the impending havoc and bloodshed, she devises a strategy to save her life and the lives of her family. And who can blame her? If the story is read from Israel's perspective, the authors write:

> Rahab is both dispossessed and repossessed. She loses her home and community in Jericho to find new ones in the midst of Israel. She is an outsider who becomes an insider, a person inhabiting the margin (a prostitute living in the city wall) who moves to the center of Israel, confusing Israel's self-identification.[40]

These readings offer a sympathetic interpretation of a loose woman stigmatized by society and struggling to survive war and violence. In following the narrator's storyline, however, Bird, Fewell, and Gunn have not read against the grain: they have not questioned the violent history of conquest and the occupation of foreign land inscribed in the text. By moving Rahab from the margin to the center, they portray the harlot as living among and assimilated into the people and culture of those who conquered her own people. This interpretation begs the question: What about the Canaanites, the multitude of Rahab's people who were killed?

Taking up the challenge to read the story from a Canaanite perspective, Native-American scholar Laura Donaldson highlights Rahab's role as the Canaanite "Other"—those people inhabiting the land before the invasion and the bloodbath. In her view, "the narrative figures of Rahab and Ruth conjure not only the position of the indigene in the biblical text but also the specific cultural and historical predicament of American Indian women."[41] She notes the persistent white fantasy in which Native women fall in love with, or befriend, the white men who have come to kill their people and take their land from them. Like Pocahontas, Rahab becomes a representative of the "good native" who acquiesces voluntarily to the conquerors, offering them protection and assistance in subduing her own people.

Building on Donaldson's reading, Lori Rowlett directs her attention not so much to Rahab as an individual victim or heroine as to the representations of gender, sexuality, and prostitution in depictions of the Other in biblical conquest narratives. She notes that prostitution is the dominant biblical image of the religions of Israel's neighbors. This is because "throughout most of the Bible, the beliefs and practices of the various ethnic groups lumped together as Canaanites are condemned as obscene."[42] The Hebrew prophets persistently admonished their people not to participate in Canaanite religions, described as "whoring after other gods." Thus, the symbol of Rahab as a converted prostitute might also signify the transformation of the land "from sexually lascivious paganism (in Hebrew eyes) to colonized docility."[43] Rowlett discerns four disturbing parallels between Rahab and the Pocahontas of Disney/popular media: the Native woman falls in love or has sex with the conqueror(s); she saves the conquerors and offers them assistance against her own people; she embraces the colonizing culture wholeheartedly; and her body and reproductive powers are co-opted in the conquest.[44]

By far the most extensive use of the Rahab story to illustrate a postcolonial feminist interpretation is Musa Dube's *Postcolonial Feminist Interpretation of the Bible*. Dube insists that subverting the patriarchal reading of the text is not sufficient without simultaneously debunking the imperial ideology inscribed within it. She suggests using "Rahab's reading prism" to scrutinize the imperialist ideology of colonizing other peoples in biblical texts and biblical interpretations of those texts. Doing so includes asking whether or not the text has a clear stance against political imperialism, encourages travel to a distance land and justifies inhabiting other peoples' land, constructs difference between different groups in unequal ways, and employs gender to construct unequal power relationships.[45] Using such a reading prism, Dube highlights "the dangers of reclaiming women's roles without naming [the texts'] imperialistic agendas."[46] In imperializing narratives, she notes, women often represent land; Rahab's story is no exception, for she reflects the colonizers' desire to enter and domesticate the land of Canaan. Echoing Rowlett's reading, Dube points out that it is not surprising that Rahab is portrayed as a prostitute, for she symbolizes the land as wild, inadequate, and waiting to be tamed by others with superior morals.[47] Instead of praising Rahab's knowledge of Deuteronomy and her faithfulness to the colonizers, Dube judges her to be a sellout, one who betrays her own people. Rahab is colonized not only bodily but also mentally, for she knows Deuteronomy better than the colonizers do.[48] Using "Rahab's reading prism," Dube highlights the different motives and interests to be found in reading strategies used by white women compared to those of women in the two-thirds world.

As a critic from Asia, where sex tourism is a flourishing business and some countries can be considered "the brothel of the world," I read Rahab's story from the perspective of women compelled to provide sexual labor as an integral part of global markets and military buildup. In southeast Asia, institutionalized prostitution began with the establishment of American military bases during the Vietnam War. American soldiers were sent to cities in southeast Asia for "rest and recreation." After the war, promoting tourism to sustain the entertainment businesses led to the formation of an institutionalized sex industry in which Asian women have to sell their bodies to men from rich nations. Sex tourism, Denise Brennan notes, "is fueled by the fantasies of white, First-World men who exoticize dark-skinned 'native' bodies in the developing world, where they can buy sex for cut-rate prices."[49] In Thailand, for example, the sex industry brought in $7.6 billion in 1995; the industry ranked third highest among reliable sources of foreign currency, leading Nantawan Broonprasat Lewis to call prostitution a new form of colonization.[50] The sex industry remains intimately linked with militarism; the sexual use of women, along with alcohol and drugs, is regarded as a necessary channel for letting off steam from military life. After the first Gulf War in 1991, for example, Manila became a stopover for "fun" before American soldiers returned home.[51]

Prostitutes in Asian cities are stigmatized by their own people as loose and unclean, for they flirt and sleep with foreigners. They live in the contact zone where bodies meet and cultures collide.

These women have relatively little protection from pimps, police, or the law. Like the harlot Rahab, prostitutes in Asia may also come from poor backgrounds and provide for dependent families. Before we rush to condemn an ancient (or modern) Rahab as a "loose woman," to lift her up as a heroine, or to reject her as a sellout, we ought to investigate the larger societal forces and global structures that join hands to keep her in her place. We should ask, What are the alternatives?

The story of Rahab reminds us of the complex layers and multiple interpretations of colonial history in which colonial subjects cannot be easily or decisively classified as heroines or villains. As Albert Memmi reminded us long ago, colonization could not have existed for so long without native collaborators.[52] Ashis Nandy has pointed to the complex psychodynamics of the colonized.[53] Rahab can be seen as epitomizing the fractured, twisted, and tormented subjectivity produced in a colonial situation, her loyalties divided and not of her choosing. Like the story of the colonized, hers is a fragmented, incoherent, and half-erased tale. Although some have conjectured that the story in its earliest oral form originated with the Rahab clan living in the ruins of Jericho,[54] the final form of the story has come down to us as redacted and told from the Israelites' perspective. Rabah's voice as a subaltern is forever lost to us, as Lori Rowlett laments: "The colonizing powers telling the story have given her words to speak in praise of themselves as conquering heroes."[55] Rahab is a complex figure; her story defies easy reading and points to the need for postcolonial intellectuals to grapple with the messiness of many layers of colonial history, its multiple inscriptions on a colonial subject, and the colonized subject's psychology of survival.

Love between Women and Imperial Values and Vices

The other kind of "loose women" I wish to consider are those outside the realm of social respectability and heterosexual normativity. As in the case of Rahab, these women did not leave behind their own writings; and their stories were narrated by others in the Bible. For example, Paul discussed them in the opening chapter of the Epistle to the Romans. As a Greek-speaking, diasporic Jew living under the domination of the Roman Empire, Paul compromised his privileges as a Pharisee and risked alienating himself from other Jewish elites by joining the Jesus movement. His remarks on homoerotic relationships in Romans 1 offer an opportunity to investigate intersections among gender, sexuality, ethnicity, religion, and empire in the politics of his time. Such a discussion is timely because debates on sexual morality, family values, and same-sex marriage are so very intertwined with American politics today.

In order to advance a postcolonial reading of Paul's teaching on homoerotic relationships between women, one must steer away from an earlier approach of trying to find proof texts in the Bible to support or condemn homosexuality. Reading the Bible with such a motive in mind easily courts the dangers of collapsing the differences among the contexts and audiences of the texts and of reading the Bible anachronistically in order to solve modern problems.[56] The people living in biblical times did not share our modern social constructions of sexual identity and orientation. Furthermore, citing the Bible as authority is never value neutral, as Robert Goss has reminded us: "The Bible has been used as a weapon of terror against gay men and lesbians." He labels those several texts used repeatedly to justify the oppression of queer people as "texts of terror."[57] At the same time, a postcolonial critic cannot focus solely on Paul's religion and theology and be preoccupied only with teasing out whether his views on sexuality were influenced by Judaism or by Hellenistic philosophy and thought. This bifurcation and polarization of Judaic and Hellenistic influence in Paul has proven inadequate for understanding his construction of his own identity and the complex interactions of cultures in his time.

A postcolonial reading of Paul must bring into sharp relief the context of the Roman Empire in which Paul lived. In his various writings and the several anthologies he has edited, Richard Horsley has presented the thought-provoking claim that Paul's Gospel is not against Judaism but the Roman imperial order.[58] Horsley argues that Paul was neither a rousing revolutionary nor a proclaimer of judgment against the Roman emperor; instead, his mission and his active engagement in forming alternative communities were in pursuit of an anti-imperial agenda. Paul's religion was not concerned only with the individual or the private sphere; it encompassed social, economic, and political consequences. Horsley explains Paul's subversive strategy in this way:

> Imperial power relations operated in complex ways through cultural-religious forms integrally related to

social-economic forms of domination, and not simply by
the sword; likewise, Paul pursued his mission in complex
cultural modes integrally related to the social formation
that he and others were catalyzing.[59]

While I support Horsley and others whose interpretations
emphasize Paul's relationship with politics in the Roman Empire,
I stress that feminist scholars, taking into consideration gender, sexuality, and ethnicity, have argued that Paul's rhetoric and
politics were more complex and cannot be construed as merely
anti-imperial.[60] First of all, scholars who have studied modern
anti-colonial and anti-imperial movements have shown that male
elites who are radical in their political views may be oblivious to
women's issues and concerns.[61] Second, because of their androcentric biases, some male scholars and interpreters disregard or
overlook the political implications of gender and sexuality. Their
interpretive framework does not take into serious account the
ways in which sexism and heterosexism perpetuate the consoli-
dation of state power. The passage in Romans 1, in which Paul
discusses explicitly female homoerotic relationships, provides us
with an interesting case through which to examine these issues in
more detail.

Most of the studies and commentaries on Rom. 1:26-27 have
been written by male scholars and reflect their own interests and
social locations. As expected, they have focused more on male
homosexuality, partly because they can allude to other passages
in the Bible that concern male same-sex relations (for example,
Lev. 18:22, 20:13), and partly because materials and resources on
female erotic love are harder to find and document. Bernadette
Brooten has charged that male biases and the lack of attention to
gender analysis lead to incomplete pictures and sometimes even
to erroneous interpretations, such as the suggestion that there
had been more tolerance of female homoerotic behaviors in the
Greco-Roman period. At the same time, female scholars working
within a "decent" paradigm (to use Althaus-Reid's terminology)
have largely overlooked female homoeroticism in their construction of women's history and gender relations.[62]

A postcolonial reading of Romans 1 benefits from insights
made possible by "Rahab's reading prism" because it insists that
we read patriarchal relations and imperial ideology together. We
need to ask what kinds of gender relationships and what sorts of

family values the Roman Empire promulgated. As the many works of Mary Rose D'Angelo have clearly demonstrated, the Roman Empire was keen on maintaining a hierarchal relation between the genders because the proper governance of the household was critical for the functioning of the imperial order.[63] Augustus initiated a "family values" campaign and sought to restore ancient mores with regard to marriage, family, and sexual morality through his marriage laws. Subsequent Roman emperors, such as Trajan and Hadrian, likewise recognized the importance of strengthening patriarchal family values and structures as a means of consolidating social control. As a vast patronage system, the Roman Empire could be seen as a large *paterfamilias*, with networks of hierarchical relationships requiring the submission of provincial elites to the imperial family. Family was an important social metaphor; the control of males over women, children, and slaves in the household defined proper masculinity and ensured the smooth running of the state.

In Rom. 1:26-27, Paul speaks of women who "exchanged natural intercourse for unnatural" and of men who gave up natural intercourse with women and were consumed with passion for other males. Scholars have not agreed about how best to interpret the words *natural* and *unnatural* in the original Greek. A few male scholars have suggested that Paul was actually condemning anal intercourse, oral sex, or other "sexual perversions" and not speaking of homosexuality.[64] Brooten, however, takes a different approach and points out that the word *nature* has two potential meanings: order or nature as established by God and the gendered nature of human beings.[65] For Paul, as for his contemporaries, nature entailed a gender hierarchy; it was against this natural order for women to exchange their passive, subordinate role for an active role. After carefully reviewing the evidence from Greek and Roman sources, Brooten concludes:

> Like the hellenistic- and Roman-period authors surveyed above, [Paul] views sexual relations as asymmetrical, so that a sexual encounter necessarily includes an active and passive partner. . . . According to this literature, a woman cannot naturally assume the active role, thus rendering natural sexual relations between women impossible.[66]

Brooten also cites 1 Cor. 11:2-16, in which Paul requires women to keep their hair long and wear a veil, to support her claim. Her focus compares Paul's position with the cultural-religious thought of his time; it does not draw out explicitly the relation between gender, sexuality, and empire. But if Paul subscribed to the gender hierarchy of his time and shared similar assumptions about female homoeroticism with his contemporaries, then it would be hard to argue that he opposed imperial family values and gender arrangements.

Interpretation of this passage is complicated because some scholars argue that Paul was not speaking about homosexuality in general. Rather, he had special targets in mind—those who did not believe in God and who worshiped human-made idols (vv. 22-23). For advocates of this view, sexuality functioned not as a marker of gender relationships, but as a religious boundary setter. For example, William Countryman interprets this passage in light of Jewish purity. He argues that Paul described homosexual acts as unclean, improper, and "over against culture" but did not use the vocabulary of sin. Paul saw the culture of Gentiles as full of vices; God had surrendered the Gentiles to homosexual behavior, which was "an integral if unpleasingly dirty aspect of Gentile culture."[67] Although Dale Martin does not focus on purity, he, too, suggests that this passage is best read against the context of condemnation of idolatry and Gentile culture. Martin rejects the idea that Paul was condemning homosexuality as part of the universal, fallen human nature. Such a reading reflects a heterosexist bias, for Paul nowhere referred to the Genesis story of Adam, Eve, Eden, and the Fall in this passage. Instead, Martin suggests, "As punishment for their invention of idolatry and polytheism, God 'handed them over' to depravity, allowing them to follow their 'passions,' which led them into sexual immorality, particularly same-sex coupling."[68] He also notes that sexual immorality and other impurities have long been used by Jewish writers to distinguish Gentile from Jewish culture.

The linkage between homosexual behavior and idolatry in Gentile cultures has allowed gay activists and their allies to argue that Paul spoke out of a particular context that cannot be applied to modern situations. Robert Goss, for example, states, "Paul presupposes a deviation from nature because of idolatry and Pharisaic purity code. His statement in Romans 1:26-27 is intertwined with his particular sociocultural context, and it does violence to Paul's perspective to apply his linkage of cultic prostitution and idolatry to the contemporary situation of queers."[69] Although I fully support the position that the Bible should not be used to oppress gay men and lesbians, I want to highlight the danger of reinscribing the view that Gentile culture was somehow sexually immoral or depraved rather than seriously questioning it. As Elisabeth Schüssler Fiorenza has warned, "The majority of scholars have followed Paul's example in reconstructing his arguments as 'normative' over and against Paul's so-called Gnostic, libertine, or Jewish legalistic 'opponents.'"[70] This dualistic logic and rhetoric has been repeatedly produced in colonial discourse to denigrate other peoples' cultures and to justify the "civilizing mission" of the West. Furthermore, missionaries have condemned indigenous sexual practices, including homosexual behaviors, as incompatible with the Bible's teachings in order to reinforce their own heterosexist teachings on marriage and sexual morality.

In an interesting article, Jennifer Wright Knust suggests that Paul's use of the language of sexual virtue and vice was subversive and different from the political rhetoric of the Roman Order. For her, the contrast Paul drew between the virtue of the brothers and sisters in Christ and the depravity of the Gentiles was a coded way of challenging Rome's imperial claims. According to the imperial propaganda and logic of Paul's time, emperors were virtuous, exceptionally self-controlled, and able to bring about harmony and well being in the Empire. In comparison, Knust argues, Paul's condemnation of sexual immorality and slavishness, as well as his citation of the list of vices in Rom. 1:29-31, was a form of anti-imperial rhetoric leveled against the prevailing order. But in making these charges, Knust says, Paul reproduced cultural assumptions of his time:

> His critique of Roman imperial pretensions, framed, in part, in terms of sexual virtue and vice, depended upon and reinscribed hierarchical theories of sex and gender historically used by Romans and Greeks to claim their privileged status while undermining the claims of their rivals.[71]

Knust's observations find support in contemporary postcolonial studies, especially in the work of Homi Bhabha, who suggests that colonized subjects are cultural hybrids with a double consciousness who may employ the language and cultural codes of their colonizers to subvert the colonial order.[72] If Paul intended to direct his rhetoric against the Empire, however, he did not give readers strong hints to read in that way. Paul's exhortation to submit to the governing authorities (Rom. 13:1-7) will also be difficult to explain. As Knust notes, because Paul replicated the cultural assumptions of gender difference and religious boundaries of his time, it would be difficult for Paul's audience to interpret him in a subversive or iconoclastic manner.

Conclusion

The investigation of "loose women" in the Bible allows us to gauge how a society defines gender relationships, sexual normativity, marriage, and friendship and love between women. A postcolonial reading will insist on placing sexuality within a wider social network of relations such as ethnicity, religion, family, economics, and politics. In the case of Rahab, the prostitute symbolizes not only the availability of her female body and reproductive power, but also the domestication of the land, the licentious behavior of the Canaanites, and the unequal position between the colonizers and the conquered. Reading Rahab as the intersection of interlocking power relations offers a reading prism through which to scrutinize other biblical texts and provides a reading that emphasizes the linkage between patriarchy and the ideologies of conquest and empire. Using some of these insights to interpret Rom. 1:26-27, I find that female homoeroticism can also serve as a prism to reflect not only power relationships within the text, but also the assumptions and presuppositions of its interpreters. Again, sexuality and gender relationships can be read in the larger contexts of the promotion of family values and enforcement of sexual regulation of the Empire, the setting of boundaries between ethnic and religious groups, and Paul's rhetoric as a Jewish religious leader in the diaspora. I highlight the tension between claims that Paul was anti-imperial and that his subscription to cultural assumptions supported and legitimate state power.

Today, when so-called family values and sexual morality occupy prominent place in American politics and threats to the family are seen by the Right as threats to the nation, the discussion of "loose women" and their bodies has particular relevance. As Janet Jakobsen has noted, "Because bodies literally are the site of intersection of various social relations—gender, race, class, as well as sexuality—sexual regulation can carry the stakes for these various relations and the social differentiation upon which they depend."[73] Interpreting "loose women" in biblical and contemporary times can illuminate the social values and norms that underlie discussions of sexuality. And discourse on sexuality, as we have seen above, can open up our understanding of the regulatory power of sex in broader social relations, as well as in the social imaginations of the interpreters.

Study Questions

1. What is your understanding of sexual morality in Christianity? How is the Bible used in shaping women's sexual morality? Has your understanding changed because of this essay? If so, how?

2. How do you understand Rahab as a woman? How do you understand her as a biblical figure? How does this relate to women in the community in which you live?—In the faith community in which you worship?

3. How does Kwok understand Rahab from her postcolonial feminist hermeneutic? How does Kwok relate the story of Rahab in terms of gender, sexuality, and power? What are the political, gender, and sexual contexts of Rahab's world?

4. How does the relationship between sexual morality and national politics play in Rahab's world compared to your own context? How do you respond to Kwok's shift of perspective from Israel to Canaanites?

5. To what further study is this essay inviting you? Is there a global setting to which you are drawn to learn and connect with the "imperial ideology of colonizing other people"?

III. A Communal Reading

See—Judge—Act

A Different Approach
to Bible Study

Aida Irizarry-Fernández

Perspective

In the Latino community, studying Scripture always offers opportunities for building community, undergoing transforming moments, and having good strong coffee at the table. I hope that when people gather for this Bible study, they will experience the first two of these goals. The caffeine part is up to you!

The methodology I wish to share is one of the teaching tools used by many facilitators in training pastor mentors and lay missioners of the National Plan for Hispanic Ministries of the United Methodist Church. This methodology was developed in 1992 by the Reverend Saul Trinidad, a dear friend whom I call the "Inca guru." Trinidad is a pastor-theologian from Peru, currently residing in San Antonio, Texas, who serves as a consultant to the General Board of Global Ministries of the United Methodist Church. His passion and deep sense of justice are reflected in the curriculum.[1] Justo González, one of our most prolific Latino scholars, has written a series of very popular Bible studies using Trinidad's methodology. His books include studies on the Gospel of John, Revelation, the Gospel of Matthew, Acts, and a few of the apostle Paul's epistles.

Among the richest characteristics of this teaching tool are fluidity and adaptability—though not at the cost of its core pedagogical principles. The See—Judge—Act methodology is an action/reflection process rooted in liberation theology and thinking. Its aim is to engender a simple, but thorough, process that helps participants broaden their theological understanding as well as their practice of ministry. It is an empowering process. The See—Judge—Act Bible study approach promotes team ministry, team analysis, and unity in the Spirit among highly diverse communities, such as the Latino/Hispanic American population in the United States. According to reports from the Office of Research and Planning of the General Council of Ministries, the Hispanic population in the United States increased from 22,585,214 in 1990 to 35,654,351 in 2004. The projection is that by the year 2010, the Latino/Hispanic community will become the largest ethnic group in the United States. The need to develop innovative and creative ways to approach this community is extraordinary. The user-friendly Bible study methodology described here attempts to reach the "unchurched." The See—Judge—Act invitational style provides an environment in which both congregation members and the "unchurched" are welcomed, embraced, and nurtured.

It is important to underscore the diversity among Latino populations currently living in the United States. Our highly multicultural and multilingual community speaks Spanish, Portuguese, English, and many indigenous dialects. In addition, the Latino population enjoys variety in taste and diet; it expresses itself variously in the arts and music; most important here, a variety of theological traditions can be found within our communities. Despite our great diversity, we still feel that we belong to the same *raza*. Virgilio Elizondo describes this conviction as "cosmic race."[2] It is not the color of our skin that brings us together as one people, for we are multiracial. Rather, we share historical memory. In one way or another, we are all children of the sufferings and pains of conquest and colonization; we are siblings in exile from the south to the north of the continent.

The goal of the See—Judge—Act method of biblical inquiry is transformation. The expectation is that those who engage in its action-reflection process will become faithful agents of change within a church and society that operate from the demands of the Reign of God. Romans 12:2 is the scriptural foundation of this teaching/learning tool. The apostle Paul writes, "Do not be conformed to this world, but be transformed by the renewing of your minds, so that you may discern what is the will of God—what is good and acceptable and perfect" (NRSV).

It is important to emphasize that this methodology does not reflect the linear thinking and value system of the Western European world; rather, it enlists the more circular movement of ideas, emotions, and values of non-Westerners. This movement is constant. The mathematical symbol for infinity (∞) serves as an appropriate sign of this movement in the action-reflection model. Antonio Machado, a Spanish poet, once wrote:

> Caminante, no hay camino,
> se hace camino al andar. . . .
> Se hace camino al andar.
>
> Sojourner, there is no path,
> the path is built as we walk. . . .
> The path is built as we walk.

Every time we come together for Bible study, a new epiphany may emerge. Such an epiphany can open the door to a new understanding of ourselves and of God. There is ample room for our relationship with the Creator and with one another to expand into a more inclusive community. "The path is built as we walk" together in community.

Another interesting feature of this methodology is its egalitarian quality. Let me explain. The emphasis on corporate learning creates a collegial atmosphere, in which participants accompany and support each other in the study of the Word. This sense of companionship allows the lay person and the clergy, the man and the woman, the youth and the adult, the heterosexual and the homosexual, the literate and the illiterate, the academic and the non-academic, the professional and the non-professional, the blind and the sighted to sit together around the same table. Each brings her or his own gifts and experiences to the realm of community. Individuals are affirmed and encouraged to express their own theological thinking in ways that will sustain, rather than divide, the community.

The Facilitator

The See—Judge—Act Bible study leader is not introduced as teacher, scholar, or expert but as facilitator of a creative process.

The facilitator is invited to use as many resources as possible to help the text come alive within the group. I like to use the image of a midwife with strong and caring hands, skillfully working through the messy birth canal. The Word is no longer safely in the womb of theological thinking. It is well, alive, crying, and kicking before the whole community, taking shape, form, and meaning.

Many who have experienced this methodology are amazed by its power. At the conclusion of a Module I training event for lay missioners, I once heard unforgettable testimony from one participant. This rather shy young man said, "I came here thinking this was going to be just another training session, but here I have felt the Holy Spirit transforming my life. I am not a scared immigrant anymore. I am a child of the Most High God."

The Methodology

Each step in the See—Judge—Act approach refers to a specific movement in the study of the Word. The facilitator can provide participants with a series of key questions to aid the group in initiating its exegetical journey.

The first step, *See*, refers simply to examining the text. This movement is an invitation to read it closely, to listen to and observe carefully the characters in the story, and to pay attention to their historical and social context(s).

Key questions: Who are the characters in this text? What is their context? Why do the characters find themselves in their present circumstances? What concerns and/or problems appear in the story? What emotions and feelings filter through the story? What do you think the author is trying to communicate to his or her community?

The second step, *Judge*, refers to spiritual discernment. This movement provides opportunities for participants to discern and analyze their own circumstances in light of the biblical text. It is an invitation to evaluate the conditions of our lives.

Key questions: How does the text speak to us, to our community, today? What is the good news? What analysis of my community do I need to do in light of this Scripture? What is God's purpose for us in light of what we have heard? Do I need to make any changes in my behavior, in my perspectives, in my way of thinking, in my praying? Do we need to reconsider corporate decisions? Are we making a difference in the life of our church, our denomination, our community, and our world? What challenges do we hear from the text and amidst our dialogue with one another?

Finally, we arrive to the last step, *Act*, which refers to transformation. In this third movement, some level of spiritual, political, or social change is anticipated. We move from reflection into action. In this step, the text is re-read and reformulated in order to assist us in moving from assessment into commitment.

Key questions: What steps do I/we need to take in order to be responsive to the invitation we hear in the text? Who needs to be involved? How are we going to implement changes? How will change affect my community, my church, and our denomination? How can we make this world a better place for the human race? How are we building the Reign of God in our midst?

It may be important to remind participants of a simple, two-pronged ground rule: we need both an *open mind* and a *willing heart* in order to truly listen to the Spirit's voice in our midst. Whether a participant is a long-term church member or a newly formed seeker, table fellowship becomes an opportunity to enter sacred ground together in a journey of faith.

The Selection of a Text

The biblical passage I want to share is well known, but it has taken on new meaning for me since I first explored it using the method of See—Judge—Act. Let me share how I rediscovered this biblical text.

Several months ago, I had a very strange dream. Not only was it weird, but I dreamed it three nights in a row! Although I could make no sense of it at the time, the dream was vivid and disturbing to me.

In my dream, I was standing in the middle of a huge, dark valley, the fog so dense I could almost cut it with a knife. In fact, in some patches of the valley, I could not even see my hands. The ground was muddy and soft under my feet, and I felt cold— strangely cold. Suddenly, I heard a noise, and a strong wind stroke my face. As I paid closer attention to the dark landscape before me, I began to see shapes emerging from the shadows and the ground. To my surprise, these shapes turned out to be steel robots that looked like human skeletons. They were approaching from the four corners of the valley, and their eyes were bright red lights. I heard voices screaming "There are too many of them; we are not going to make it!"

I felt overwhelmed by sadness and fear. As I moved forward, the dense fog began to envelope me, like a snake ready to suffocate its prey. For a moment, I was disoriented. Then I saw people running, trying to get away from the robots. Some of those touched by the robots became like them; others died.

I was desperate. I slowly turned around and realized I was not alone: a group of people were with me. They looked somewhat sleepy. I shouted to the crowd, "Awake, rise up, we must find the brain that controls those robots and destroy it. Don't despair, we will be saved." People began to wake up. We moved toward the adversary. I shouted again, "We have no weapons in our hands, but victory is ours."

I woke up all sweaty and anxious. I did not mention my dream to anyone. I just recorded it in my journal, planning to share it later with my spiritual director. Well, time passed by; my dreams moved to the back burner of my mind, and I forgot about them.

Let me tell you, God has a very particular sense of humor! Perhaps a month after my dream, I escaped to the movies—the only place where I get no interruptions, since cell phones are not permitted. Suddenly, I was interrupted—not by a cell phone, or by a person, but by a movie trailer on the theater screen. I was looking at part of my dream! Actually, it was a preview of Arnold Schwarzenegger's film *Terminator Part III: The Rise of the Machine*.

I must confess that watching part my dream on the big screen was both alarming and comical. I simply asked God, "What are you trying to tell me? You have my full attention!"

Later, at a retreat, prayer about my dream guided me to Ezek. 37:1-14. I wrestled with this text over and over again. Ezekiel did not have the same technology we have today. In his vision, he saw scattered piles of human bones. In my dream, I saw shiny steel robots with red eyes.

See

The hand of the Lord came upon me, and he brought me out by the spirit of the Lord and set me down in the middle of a valley; it was full of bones. He led me all round them; there were very many lying in the valley, and they were very dry. He said to me, "Mortal, can these bones live?" I answered, "O Lord God, you know." Then he said to me, "Prophesy to these bones, and say to them: O dry bones, hear the word of the LORD. Thus says the Lord GOD to these bones: I will cause breath to enter you, and you shall live. I will lay sinews on you, and will cause flesh to come upon you, and cover you with skin, and put breath in you, and you shall live; and you shall know that I am the LORD."

So I prophesied as I had been commanded; and as I prophesied, suddenly there was a noise, a rattling, and the bones came together, bone to its bone. I looked, and there were sinews on them, and flesh had come upon them, and skin had covered them; but there was no breath in them. Then he said to me, "Prophesy to the breath, prophesy, mortal, and say to the breath: Thus says the Lord GOD: Come from the four winds, O breath, and breathe upon these slain, that they may live." I prophesied as he commanded me, and the breath came into them, and they lived, and stood on their feet, a vast multitude.

Then he said to me, "Mortal, these bones are the whole house of Israel. They say, 'Our bones are dried up, and our hope is lost; we are cut off completely.' Therefore prophesy, and say to them, "Thus says the Lord GOD: I am going to open your graves, and bring you up from your graves, O my people; and I will bring you back to the land of Israel. And you shall know that I am the LORD, when I open your graves, and bring you up from your graves, O my people. I will put my spirit within you, and you shall live, and I will place you on your own soil; then you shall know that I, the LORD, have spoken and will act, says the LORD." (Ezek. 37:1-14; NRSV)

Ezekiel's vision was not a pretty sight. Between you and me, I suspect author Stephen King draws some inspiration from Ezekiel's brilliant and highly unusual writings. We cannot deny he was a master of metaphor. Although some scholars have tried to psychoanalyze and diagnose Ezekiel as unstable, and perhaps even a little bit crazy, because of his eccentric and bizarre imagery, I think he was absolutely brilliant. I agree with those who say he was in a league of his own. His writings are intense, filled with emotion and passion, rich and fascinating drama. They are like psychological thrillers: while reading, you must maintain your focus—otherwise, you might miss important clues.

Ezekiel knows his audience's pain. They are living in exile, suffering under the reign of the able but determined King Nebuchadnezzar, who stopped at nothing to subdue rebellious peoples and nations within his mighty empire.

Biblical scholars agree that the prophet's personal life, as revealed in the book bearing his name, was afflicted by trials and painful losses. They report that after his wife's sudden death, he was unable to mourn his loss through customary rituals. Perhaps his emotional state is reflected in the darkness of some of his writings.

Though the text does not describe Ezekiel in psychological terms, I believe he was an introvert who suffered from emotional problems. He spent great amounts of time secluded in his home, and yet we know him as one of the Old Testament's greatest prophets. For me, his story may be used as a message of hope, particularly for those who are afflicted or who live with emotional and/or physical disabilities. Despite their problems, God can use them in powerful ways. Thus, the invitation for those suffering from depression is to avoid falling into the pit of self-pity and paralysis.

Ezekiel's famous vision of the valley of dry bones (Ezek. 37:1-14) is one of four major vision reports in his book. The others appear in Ezekiel 1–3, 8:1—11:25, and 40:1—48:35. Each of these vision reports has been subjected to much scrutiny and interpretation. Most interpreters of the Bible agree that such powerful and dramatic imagery functions to capture the attention of Ezekiel's audience—those exiles who resided in Babylonia for years before Jerusalem was actually destroyed and who lamented their tragic circumstances. Their hope had perished; they felt totally helpless and dry. Because Ezekiel's previous oracles included so many words of judgment and condemnation for sin, the exiles felt as if they were already in the grave. They existed as the walking dead.

How can you summon someone's attention in such a depressive state? Perhaps this is what the vision of the valley of dry bones was all about: an outside-the-box, illogical intervention. The passage is filled with promise—a vision of renewal and restoration for the people of Israel.

After carefully reading the text, I envision an ugly and desolated battlefield filled with unburied bones, dust, and silence. I see Ezekiel standing in the middle of this "death valley," then moving about, astonished by the image before his eyes. I see him confused, not knowing what to expect next. Caught up in his vision, Ezekiel suddenly hears God's voice. He receives the command to prophesy to the heaps of lifeless bones, to announce that they shall live again! Without questioning God, he does as he is told. We can only admire Ezekiel for not fleeing from such a terrifying scenario, though he might have been scared to death. The prophet remains determined to fulfill his newly appointed mission. As he shouts God's life-giving words, the bones around him begin to rattle, shake, and re-member—each to its appropriate bone. Ezekiel stands firm, and together we witness the impossible becoming possible. Natural laws of life and death are broken. Logic plays no part in the unfolding events in this vision. I see bone to bone, tissue to tissue, nerve to nerve, skin racing to cover the muscles of what appear to be human bodies, a whole mass of them. The prophet still stands in awe of what he is witnessing. Then, another miracle takes place: the bodies receive the breath of life. They are no longer lifeless corpses but breathing creatures enlivened by the power of the Spirit. These are no zombies, wondering why they have not yet been reduced to dust. No, these are new creatures brought forth for a purpose. Now, Ezekiel stands in the valley, where the sun has dissipated all darkness and light shines through. The prophet smiles; perhaps he lifts a prayer of thanksgiving for not running away in panic from the first things he saw.

Judge

This text invites us to read it over and over again. The prophet's vision triggers provocative thoughts and raises crucial questions for twenty-first-century readers. It is speaking to me as never before. Why has Ezekiel's vision touched me so deeply, as if I were seeing and listening to him right then and there?

The answer to my question emerges slowly from the depth of my soul. Ezekiel's vision of the valley of dry bones has become my vision, too, by the power of the transcendent Word. His vision is a message for today, a message of hope for the Latino people, *un mensaje de esperanza para el pueblo Latino*, in the United States. The vision of the desolated valley of dry bones is also a vision of the bones of Latino ancestors who came to this country and died in exile. They suffered from and mourned the fact that they were never able to return to their beloved homelands.

The text moves me to think that this valley of dry bones is also the valley of dry dreams, unfulfilled expectations, and broken promises. Many came with so much faith, wishing and praying for a better life, but instead found rejection and bitterness. They encountered the lords of racism and classism, who tried to smash their dignity without compassion.

The dry bones are indeed scattered all over the valley. These are the bones of many of our brothers and sisters whose hopes were meticulously dismembered by the ax of sharp oppression and exploitation. Many suffered in silence; others were silenced by the indifference of groups and agencies.

The resilience of Latino communities is admirable. Despite much pain and disillusionment, they always hope for a better *mañana* (tomorrow). "What else could go wrong?" is a rhetorical question I often hear in the midst of crises. This question always receives the same response, "Do not lose heart; *mañana* will be a better day." Such conversations might suggest an element of fatalism in Latino/Hispanic culture. Whether or not this perception is accurate, I suggest that these conversations speak of a people of deep faith. People who scream, cry, and even throw temper tantrums in response to life's trials in one moment will, in the next, laugh, joke, and even dance. "Life is too short" is the philosophy of many; "*Mañana* is always better."

In the midst of this resilient attitude, however, we cannot deny our historical memories of a cruel past. Our mixed blood reminds us how the Spanish, English, and Portuguese conquistadores raped our Inca, Azteca, and Taína grandmothers. We sadly hear how European colonizers brutally enslaved our African grandfathers. In both the rich African continent and the Americas, natives offered the precious gift of hospitality to strangers who wore helmets on their heads. In return, the strangers showed us their swords and chained our hospitable hands.

Latino people in the United States are often bitterly reminded of how the Eurocentric "Uncle Sam" has castrated the hopes of many of our parents. These reminders usually appear in federal or state legislation reducing benefits for the poor. Too frequently dreams are shattered for the immigrant community. Since September 11, 2001, many Latinos have come to believe that the development of a new kind of persecution has emerged against the immigrant community. They have often been mistaken for terrorists. They have been perceived as threats to home land security. On December 16, 2005, the House of Representatives passed the Border Protection, Anti-Terrorism, and Illegal Immigration Control Act.

Los huesos secos de nuestro amado y sufrido Pueblo están ciertamente esparcidos por toda esta nación. The dry bones of our beloved and suffering People are indeed spread all over this nation.

Throughout the years, the Latino charter church and mission[3] in the United States have served as a safe sanctuary for thousands of people who are not recorded in our conventional statistical reports. The church has been a place where those in exile can reclaim a sense of identity and belonging. Latino men and women have found a place, a safe dwelling for their tired souls. The local congregation has become a shelter where we can hear the Word in our native tongues, and where our spirits can dance to the joyful rhythms and tunes of the tambourine, the conga and the guitar, the flute, and the Inca harp. The Latino/Hispanic congregation is that sacred space where you can pour out your soul and be consoled, and where we can speak our mind and be understood.

In my understanding of Ezekiel's passage, I hear a clear invitation to claim it as *our* own vision—a vision of restoration and of spiritual and socio-political renewal for the Latinos and all people who dare to have faith.

We cannot be oblivious to what is happening in our midst. I strongly believe that in this new millennium, we are witnessing the birth of a new *raza latina* in the Northern hemisphere—a new *raza* whose spiritual input will be crucial to the survival of Christianity in this part of the world.

In his book, *The Next Christendom: the Coming of Global Christianity*,[4] Phillip Jenkins avers that "Hispanic presence has radically altered the nature of U.S.A. Catholicism. . . . Among first generation Latinos, Catholics massively outnumber Protestants, by 74 to 18 percent, but among the third generation, they have shrunk to 59 percent. But whatever the exact denominational balance maybe, the changing racial picture is only going to strengthen overall Christians numbers." I say "Amen" to Jenkins.

"Mortal, can these bones live?" Ezekiel is asked this question over and over again. For me, its repetition functions not to increase doubt and frustration before an impossible task but to emphasize the work of faith in the midst of so much destruction and death. Re-reading the text almost prompts my ears to hear the rumblings, to feel the earthquake. Can you hear it too? Is the ground shaking under your feet?

As the Latino community grows larger and larger, those bones are coming together, developing tendons and muscles. As the community matures in this country, new flesh, blood, and skin cover the dry bones in the valley.

Profeta, Podran estos huesos revivir?
Prophet, can these bones be revived?

Throughout the years, God has been sending prophets to our communities to restore a sense of hope and identity. Cesar Chavez, Justo González, Yolanda Pupo Ortíz, Ada María Isasi Díaz, Harold Recinos, and Minerva Carcaño are just a few of the names that come to mind. I believe communities can mention other, not so well known prophets who have touched their lives with a fresh and restoring message of hope. Many other Latino men and women have committed themselves to lead their people to wholeness.

Our children are listening to their ancestral history. The latest generation of Hispanic Americans is becoming more aware of the dangers and trials of the immigrants who are constantly crossing the frontier in search of jobs to help the families left behind. These youngest Latinos in the United States are fully bilingual, fully bicultural, and no longer hide behind perfect English. However, there are still places where people lose their jobs if they are caught speaking in Spanish.

Teachers have told parents to make an effort to speak English at home. A friend of mine in his late fifties, a very well-educated and brilliant man, once told me that his father used to say to him, "You must learn good English. Forget about Spanish. It will do no good to you. We are never returning back home." Very few of his friends know that this man has a Latino heritage. What do you think such a suggestion does to one's psychological makeup, one's soul?

In his book *Latinos in the United States: The Sacred and the Political*, David T. Abalos made a statement that remains very relevant almost twenty years later. Abalos argued, "The bottom line is that some form of bilingual/bicultural education is a non-negotiable right to help the Latino children acquire the educational develop-ment necessary to survive in the United States. Bilingual/bicul-tural education is not separation but *mestizaje*, the blending and enrichment of two ways of life and linguistic expressions."[5]

Abalos was convinced that bilingual/bicultural programming would not only benefit the immigrant population but also enrich an already "monolingual and culturally impoverished society."[6] He proposed that educating and taking care of the next gen-eration of children of color "is in America's own best economic interest in an era of global competition."[7] In other words, the con-tributions of a supported, educated, and multilingual population could lead to a fair management of resources, profitable overseas economic exchange, and better international relationships. The message previous generations received was "Your language is not good enough; your culture and your religion are deficient." The fight continues wherever municipalities and states vote to elimi-nate bilingual education from schools. We need to help our chil-dren feel proud of their ancestors, to make an effort to teach them about their lavish history. We need to let them know about their ancestors' legacy.

We must take a closer look at our evangelistic strategies whenever anyone insists that such strategies should develop inside of new Latino faith communities in the same ways that they do within other ethnic groups, or according to white Anglo-Saxon models. The concept "one size fits all" does not fit the Latino community—not even within the Latino community itself. We are a heterogeneous people with myriad, complex needs.

Act

Ezekiel's vision of the valley of dry bones is an invitation to refor-mulate my ministry, to think about new strategies to reach those who need a word of encouragement.

The words "Come from the four winds, O Breath, and breathe into these slain that they may live" keep echoing in my soul.

In my re-reading of Ezekiel's vision report, I hear a summons for the church to continue to be instrumental in the development of this old/new identity as children of the almighty God, who speaks many languages. I believe our commitment as disciples of Christ is to help our children and grandchildren be restored from the violent evangelism of the conquistadores and from the castrating enculturation of some missionaries.

Latinos need to stand up as a united community with one voice, all the while recognizing, respecting, and affirming their heterogeneous origins. Ezekiel's vision is a vision of promise and hope in which

This new multilingual and multicultural Latino People
   Is affirmed by its precious heritage and family values,
This new multilingual and multicultural Latino People
   Is blessed by its indomitable free spirit.
This new multilingual and multicultural Latino People
   Is sustained by its incredible resilience in the midst of chaos.
This new multilingual and multicultural Latino People
   Is nurtured by its irresistible faith in Jesus Christ.

Come from the four winds, O Breath, and breathe into these bones that they may live. Yes, Sí, come, Holy Spirit, and fill your people once more!

Ezekiel's vision shows me how the valley of dry bones can be transformed into a valley of life. This is no longer the land of the dead but the land of the living. The land is filled with the young blood of millions of men and women who seek every opportunity to bring justice, who keep forgiving a bloody past, but who will not allow history to repeat itself.

The Latino People is writing its new Acts for the twenty-first century. The Breath of God has breathed new life into dry bones. This is our legacy to Christianity in the new millennium—a deep faith that is not afraid to speak the truth, love the Lord passionately, and give its life for justice.

Am I too optimistic? Am I too idealistic? Perhaps; but in the dream I have described, I was inviting others to join me, to find the brain that was destroying the people in the valley of death. Those robots, I have come to understand, were the evil product of oppression and imperialism, whose victims were left to dry under the sun. I am committed to building the vision of a new land—God's promise to you and me—where there is no violence, only the power of God in each one of us. It is with our personal and corporate commitment to denounce the sophisticated but lethal conspiracy of the evil mentality that we can truly bring restoration into our midst.

Our community is growing and multiplying; genocide is no longer permitted to claim its victims. The new generation of Latinos/Hispanic Americans claims this land as its home, too, for it knows no other home. This is where we have buried our loved ones, given birth to new generations, baptized our children in the name of *el Padre, el Hijo y el Espíritu Santo*: The Father, the Son, and the Holy Spirit. This is the land where our children, our grandchildren, and our great-grandchildren have racially and ethnically mixed marriages.

This is the land where our descendents must make their dreams and hopes come true. This is the land where we must lobby for Spanish and other languages to be taught freely in public school systems so we can build better relationships in our global village, strengthen communities, and live in the spirit of Pentecost.

A new vision has emerged. It is a beautiful valley of life. Take a close look: the valley is about to burst forth with many fruits in science, medicine, education, politics, arts, economics, and technology. Showers of dignity, respect, self-worth, and justice are washing away the pollution of selfish individualism, low self-esteem, and oppression.

It is a beautiful valley of life. Take a close look: you may find yourself dancing in its meadow.

Come from the four winds, O Holy Spirit, breathe into us that we may believe and live.

Reading Biblical Narratives Imaginatively

Can we play and have fun studying Holy Scripture?

In the following pages, I invite you to play with two different biblical texts. Yes, you read correctly: I wrote *play*. To the scholars among you, I ask your forgiveness, for I understand that studying the Word is serious business. But please allow me to try a different approach. After all, you have plenty of opportunities to be very serious and formal in the classroom!

According to *Webster's Dictionary*, one of the definitions of *play* is "unconstrained activity and freedom of movement." My invitation is to the unconstrained use of your imagination. I will make some specific suggestions here for a study and discussion program, but the most important one is this: let the Holy Spirit

move freely in your midst as you explore the Word and seek out
its relevance for us today.

Perhaps a preparatory question would be helpful: "Do we need
to bring any toys to our playful time together?" Well, that is up to
you. However, let me suggest several items. First, look in that cor-
ner of your memory, the place where you left a sack full of treasures
from your childhood. Go on—open that dusty sack and search for

> a thirst for adventure,
> a risky dare,
> a deep sense of curiosity,
> a willingness to create new rules for an old game.

Your childhood memory sack likely contains much more than
these. It is all right to pull out that quick readiness to run after a
treasure hunt. After all, you never know what you might discover
behind the written Word. You may also bring

> enthusiasm,
> encouragement, and
> wisdom to share with one another.

Oh, I almost forgot! Do remember to bring your sharp sense
of taste to the playground. In your encounter with the Word, you
might taste some bittersweet candy; someone might even offer
one of those big, hard jawbreakers!

In addition to all these toys, I suggest that you also bring as
many art supplies as you can find, including construction paper,
crayons, markers, scissors, molding clay, glitter, glue, paint,
brushes, and so forth. You might even include some dry items
from the food pantry, such as beans, pasta, and cereal. The larger
the variety of art supplies and artistic expression, such as role play,
music, and dance that you bring, the greater the opportunity for
all participants to use multiple intelligences in the learning process. The objective is to make studying Scripture unforgettable.

The deployment of imagination and the creative skills of participants increase the transforming moment not only for the individual but also for the group as a whole. This approach declares that
learning is a collective as well as an individual, a spiritual as well as
an intellectual process. After all, imagination and creativity are gifts
from God, so why not use them creatively and responsibly?

The "See—Judge—Act" methodology I have described is also the name of our Bible study game. I suggest two simple requirements for those who decide to play: an open mind and a willing heart! We need to be cognizant that we bring with us a wealth of experiences derived from our cultural heritage and upbringing. Some of our childhood memories are very pleasant; others are so painful that they block or interfere with the development of new insights. For these reasons, we need to bring open minds and willing hearts. If you are receptive to these two requirements, I believe you will not regret the experience.

The two texts I have selected for our Bible study are 2 Kings 2:1-14 and Mark 14:3-9. (For a small session, I suggest inviting half of the participants to read Mark's story of the anointing at Bethany and the other half to read the story of the passing of Elijah's mantle in 2 Kings.) These two very different passages allow us to explore how Scripture connects us all with an invisible, divine thread. The ancient story and our story provide material for writing a brand new testament that may inspire, guide, and transform generations to come.

See

See refers to the simple examination of the text. This first movement is an invitation to look closely at the text, to listen carefully to characters in the story, and to learn about the text's historical context, if possible. (If you have commentaries in your church library, use them. They will prove to be a helpful resource.)

Key questions: Who are the characters? What is the context of the story? How did events/characters arrive at their present circumstances and/or conclusion? What is the concern or problem presented in the story? What emotions filter through the story? What do you think the author is trying to communicate to his or her community?

1. First reading: listen to the story as if you were listening for the first time.

2. Second reading: imagine yourself as an invisible guest in the location where the story takes place.

3. Retell the story in your own words, based on what you have seen through the eyes of your imagination. Use the key questions as guides for building your story.

Group A: Mark 14:3-9

Setting the context:
The biblical story we are about to "play" with is one of the most well known passages in the New Testament. Gospel songs, plays, poetry, and books have been inspired by this story. Jesus is making his way to Jerusalem to celebrate the Passover Seder, as was Jewish custom. The Passover is a festival in which the Jewish community remembers its deliverance from Egyptian captivity and slavery. In Jesus' day, the nationalist feeling around the time of Passover was very intense, and traveling in such a volatile atmosphere was dangerous. Jesus' preaching and teaching not only addressed the people's spiritual needs but also assessed the socio-economic and political circumstances of his time. His charismatic leadership attracted people from all avenues of life, but his challenging agenda was not popular among some political and religious figures. Those who felt threatened by Jesus watched him carefully. In fact, the high priests and religious officers were crafting an opportunity to seize and kill him.

The event at Simon's home sets the stage for Jesus' passion. He has reached a point of no return. We can imagine, therefore, that Jesus in our story is physically tired, emotionally exhausted, and has a very heavy heart.

Practice the steps already outlined: read the story twice, then retell it in your own words.

I offer you my own retelling of the story in Mark 14:3-9 as an illustration:

> Jesus is visiting a friend, Simon, a man who has had leprosy, who invited Jesus to come to his house out of gratitude for his miraculous healing. Many curious people, invited and uninvited, have gathered at the house and are engaged in animated conversation about this miracle worker.
>
> In the midst of their conversations, a woman arrives at the house. Her name is not given. Without paying attention to the others in the room, she goes directly to Jesus, who is sitting by the dining table. The woman holds tightly in her hands an alabaster jar of oil. She generously pours the exquisite oil over Jesus' head. For a few moments,

everyone falls silent. Then, as the delightful fragrance fills the room, a few who cannot hold their tongues begin to complain.

It isn't every day that someone, particularly a woman, arrives with an expensive perfume and pours it over a man's head! The people say to one another, "What a waste of money! The oil in that jar could have been sold to feed the poor in this neighborhood, so many of whom have no work." They talk about the women as if she were not there. After they finish complaining to each other, they scold her harshly. But the woman could not care less what they say. She has done what she had to do.

After Jesus recuperates from the shock of what has happened and composes himself, he says, "Stop scolding her; why are you so upset? Are you so self-absorbed, so attached to your own opinions, that you do not pay attention to the true meaning of all this? The poor are your responsibility; you are the ones who need to find ways to help them. The money from the perfumed oil might have been a short-term help, but the poor need more than alms. But what this woman has done will last forever. She has ministered to me in a very special way. She has prepared my way toward eternity. Tell everyone what she has done today, not as gossip, but as part of spreading good news, and I pray no one ever forgets what she has done today. Her story will be repeated over and over in memory of her."

What Biblical Scholarship Tells Us About This Text

According to some biblical scholars,[8] the anonymous woman in this story is its main protagonist. Mark's gospel often keeps women nameless, perhaps to avoid being too controversial or because readers expect most women to play unimportant roles.

The woman with the alabaster jar interrupts a meal at the house of Simon, a man who has had leprosy. Scholars suggest that although she is not a guest at this gathering, her presence alone has not caused turmoil. Rather, her actions have generated the others' surprise. There is no doubt that the value of the perfume—approximately one laborer's yearly salary—could have provided at least some economic relief to a few of the poor in the community. However, the author of this Gospel wants to emphasize another kind of charitable act.

Simon hosts Jesus in his home. He is another voiceless character in the story, but he is not anonymous. The Scripture does not state explicitly whether or not he had been healed of his leprosy. If not, then Jesus broke the law, since people were not allowed to have contact with his host's marginalized, outcast class. In fact, one may assume that Simon has been healed, for Jesus is not his only guest; comments made about the woman by other men in the room reflect their knowledge of Jewish law.

The complainers in the room may have been legitimately concerned by the waste or the inappropriate use of the costly oil. Observe, however, that no one in the story, including Jesus, questions the woman's motivations and behavior. Jesus could easily have asked her, "Woman, why are you doing this?" But Jesus apparently knows her intentions in his heart. Although his response implies that the righteous must fulfill their responsibilities to the poor, he allows this woman to prepare his body for burial while he is still alive. Fully aware of what is going on, he receives her gift graciously; moreover, he attempts to explain her actions to the entire group. Do they understand his explanation? There is no evidence from the text that they did.

Group B: 2 Kings 2:1-14

Setting the context:

The "passing of the mantle" story is another well known biblical passage in the Christian community. The text has been used often at the Service of Remembrance at Annual Conferences of the United Methodist Church. This worship service includes a celebration of the lives of laity and clergy who have passed to meet their Creator in heaven, as well as the passing of liturgical symbols by those who are retiring to those who will be ordained during the annual session. It is a ritual filled with deep emotions and silent prayers. The idea behind this moving ritual is to encourage the new leadership to continue a faithful and fruitful ministry. The possibility that you, my readers, may be responding to God's call to ministry, either as lay persons or as ordained clergy, inspired me to select this text. Perhaps your call is to mentor someone whom God has introduced into your life.

Two prophets, Elijah and Elisha, have been together for a while as mentor and protégé. One assumes their journey has included many teaching moments, great conversations, and embarrassing moments. The passage we are just about to recreate comes at the end of their long relationship. Again, practice these steps: read the story twice, then tell it in your own words. I offer my own retelling as an illustration.

> Two friends, Elijah and Elisha, are traveling together. They are almost at the end of their journey, because God is about to take Elijah up into heaven. Elijah, Elisha's master, mentor, and friend, says to Elisha: "Stay here; the Lord has sent me to Bethel."

> Elisha responds immediately, "You must be kidding! I have no plan to let you go alone; I will stay with you forever—well, as long as you live." The two friends continue their journey to Bethel.

> These two men are not alone, however. A group of prophets is following them. One asks Elisha, "Do you have any idea what's going on? Do you know the Lord is taking Elijah away from you today?"

> "Of course I know," Elisha responds with a heavy heart. "I don't want to talk about it."

> Again, Elijah suggests that his friend remain behind: "Elisha, please stay here. The Lord is sending me to Jericho."

> With no hesitation, the younger prophet responds to his dear mentor: "I've already told you I will never leave you. As long as you live, I'll be with you." Again, the two men follow the road to Jericho.

> Yet another of the prophets following them asks, "Elisha, do you know the Lord is taking your master from you today?"

In a very sad voice Elisha responds, "I know. Believe me, I know. But I do not want to talk about it."

Again, Elijah says to Elisha, "Stay here; the Lord has sent me to Jordan."

"For the third time, I tell you," Elisha replies, "I will never leave you. As long as you live, I'll be with you." They continue walking together toward Jordan, followed by about fifty prophets. These prophets watch in silence as the two men stand before the Jordan River. Everything is quiet except the murmur of the waters. Elijah takes his mantle, rolls it up, and strikes the water, creating a dry path for them to cross to the other side.

On the other side of the Jordan River, Elijah asks his loyal disciple: "Tell me what I can do for you before I am taken away from you."

Elisha responds quickly, as if he has been pondering this question and already knows his answer. "I want a double portion of your spirit."

"Umm," the powerful prophet replies, "what you are asking is not a small thing. However, if you see me when I am taken away from you, it will be yours. Otherwise, it will not happen."

Elijah knows Elisha will be there, of course, because Elisha has said "I will never leave you" over and over.

As they are walking and talking, a chariot of fire and horses appear. The chariot takes Elijah up into heaven in a whirlwind. Elisha watches, amazed, as Elijah disappears beyond the clouds. He cries out in grief, "My father! My father! The chariots and horsemen of Israel." Then he tears his clothes in two, as was the custom for those mourning the lost of a beloved one.

Eventually, Elisha takes Elijah's mantle from the ground where it has fallen and stands before the Jordan River.

Like his master, he strikes the water with the mantle, asking, "Where is now the Lord, the God of Elisha?" Immediately, the waters part; he crosses the river bed to the other side.

A Brief Introduction to What the Commentaries Say about Our Text

Elisha, a prophet from the Northern Kingdom of Israel, is the main character in our story. His prophetic ministry lasted about fifty years, during the reigns of Kings Joram, Jehu, Jehoahaz, and Joash. The prophet Elijah is his mentor. Scholars describe Elisha as a man of wisdom and a miracle worker. He ministered to his nation in times of crisis and helped individuals in times of need. At the moment of his calling, he left behind his farming tools and his land and became what I would call an "urban prophet." Although his mentor, Elijah, had lived in caves and deserts, Elisha preferred to reside in cities.

In addition to Elijah and Elisha, other characters appear in our story. The "company [or 'sons'] of the prophets" probably refers to a prophetic guild. Prophets flourished for a long time in Israel's Northern Kingdom and were deeply involved in the overthrow of some of its royal dynasties.

Elisha's request for a "double portion" of Elijah's spirit alludes to the legal right of the first-born son to inherit a double portion of his father's possessions (Deut. 21:15-17). Although Elisha is not literally Elijah's first-born son, he is Elijah's successor.

According to Israelite history, prophets performed important religious and social functions. They were a regular part of public life. They did not carry out their activities in isolation but as integral members of their societies. Some prophets ("central intermediaries") functioned as liaisons between God and the king and/or the temple personnel as representatives of the people as a whole. They supported orderly change in the status quo, sometimes working from the inside as the king's advisors and confidants. Other prophets ("peripheral intermediaries")[9] worked from outside the corridors of power to overthrow the status quo, calling into question even the king's actions and opposing what they regarded as unjust social policies and practices. These prophets advocated radical social change. They saw themselves as agents of moral and ethical reform.

Elisha, like his mentor, was an activist prophet, heavily involved in the politics of his time. His agenda demanded recognition of God's sovereignty and justice. The prophet did not shy from denouncing the cruelty and apostasy of some kings; rather, he confronted them passionately, risking his life in the process.

Another interesting feature of this story is its reference to a "chariot of fire" and "horses of fire" (2 Kings 2:11). In Israel's ancient world, armies used chariots to transport soldiers and their heavy equipment. Chariots were symbols of power in which kings rode. Fire was a common symbol for holiness, protection, and divine presence. So we might conclude that the "chariot of fire" that took Elijah both affirms and seals his ministry and foreshadows the kind of prophetic ministry that Elisha would experience. This newly empowered prophet would then engage in Israel's "holy" wars—that is, wars in which Israel's God fought alongside the people of Israel against their enemies.

We can summarize this story in one sentence: one prophet departs the earth to be with God, and another is initiated into God's service to Israel. For the authors of Kings, it was important to record this event in order to legitimize Elisha as the new prophetic leader of Elijah's guild.

Judge

Judge refers to spiritual discernment. This movement provides an opportunity for discerning and analyzing our own circumstances in light of the biblical text.

Key questions: How might the text speak to us and to our communities today? What is its good news? What analysis of my community do I need to do in light of this Scripture? What is God's purpose for us in light of what we have heard? Do I need to make any changes in my behavior, in my perspectives, in my way of thinking, in my praying? Do we need to reconsider corporate decisions? Are we making a difference in the life of our churches, our denominations, our communities, and our world? What challenges do you hear from the text and from your dialogue with one another?

Group A

1. Reread the text.
2. Using the art supplies, try to create a visual interpretation of the text you have read. As you create your artwork, be fully aware of your thoughts and emotions.
3. Answer the key questions. You may wish to add your own questions to the list.
4. Share your experience with the larger group.

Group B

1. Reread the text.
2. Pair yourself with a partner for a visualization exercise. Imagine the two of you in the middle of a field. A river flows in front of you; behind you, a small crowd of friends follows at a distance. One of you is Elijah, and the other is Elisha. You know that at any moment, you will be separated from one another; your long, intense relationship on earth will end.
3. Listen to the murmuring sounds around you—sounds of the river, the crowd, or perhaps of an approaching whirlwind. Speak to each other as if you really were Elijah and Elisha. What do you tell each other? What might be God's purpose for your life at this moment? As you play your role, be aware of your feelings and emotions. Remember to stay in your roles as Elijah and Elisha.
4. Answer some of the key questions identified above.
5. Share your experience with the larger group.

The following mosaic of phrases represents responses that emerged when two groups engaged in these exercises, then shared their results:

Group A

What is the invitation?
   Am I included?
      She became Jesus' priest.
         Proud me—can I be his priest too?

The call is not to be silent.
Be glad to be different.
Broken vessel in many pieces
Large and small, it made no difference.
Broken vessel leads from exclusion to inclusion,
From individual to communion.

One and all are blessed,
Blessed by the smell.
Holy action no one else dared,
Hospitality given and received.

She found her voice, we have a voice.
A lesson not to fear.
Move on, steady, firm, one goal.

Broken and blessed, could this be possible?
Where did she get the perfume?
Does it really matter?
Willingness to stand up to leadership.

Listening,
Paying attention,
Looking, talking, supporting,
Healing and restoration, holiness and wholeness.

Group B

Journey and transition
God was there,
God is still here.
Realizing God's presence in my life
Blessed twice, blessed many times
Separation, moving on

Transition from one leader to another
Courage to find your own authority
Acknowledging our own transitions
Knowing your boundaries
Fitness for leadership
Loyalty, trust, love

Overcoming the boundaries
Moving beyond

Reflections

Elisha persistently followed his mentor and friend until Elijah's departure. He was determined to journey with his teacher until the end. Elisha was determined to be blessed by his mentor, no matter what. Apparently, the blessing of his predecessor was essential to his own ministry. Elisha probably thought of the big shoes he had to fill. Therefore, he requested a double blessing, a double sense of assurance that he was capable of carrying out the task facing him. He requested a confirmation of his prophetic role. After all, he had to be accountable to the community Elijah was leaving behind. His persistence was not motivated by a thirst for power but by a full acknowledgement of the extraordinary responsibility before him after the departure of his teacher. He knew it was his turn to lead and to teach others, and he was willing to do so. But he also wanted to be well-equipped for the task.

Elijah's repeated insistence that Elisha stay behind is an interesting aspect of the story. It reminded one group of another story found in the Gospels. There appear to be some parallels between Elijah and Elisha's conversation, on one hand, and Jesus and Peter's dialogue after Jesus' resurrection, on the other. Three times, Elijah told Elisha to stay behind. Jesus asked Peter three times, "Do you love me?" Each time, Elisha said to Elijah, "I will not leave you." Peter said, "I love you" after each question. We do not know if Elijah wished to avoid the pain of the departure or if he was testing Elisha before turning his job over to him. One might suggest that the motivation behind such repetition is providing the reader with validation of Elisha's and Peter's ministries. Both Elisha and Peter were assured that their task was not their own invention: the mission ahead was not a personal agenda but God's plan for their lives.

Elisha needed to be ready for his transition. We need to prepare for our own changes, as well. Stepping into the shoes of a great leader is always difficult. However, this should not become an excuse to avoid planning ahead. The participants in this Bible study strongly affirmed that "smooth" transition does not mean "easy" transition. Transition always entails change, and change always produces anxiety. One participant said, "In order to succeed in my new appointment, I must know my boundaries well." Boundaries are about which lines to cross and which not to cross; they are about knowing your gifts and your limitations. Another participant said, "It requires knowing yourself." In family systems theory, one might say it is about becoming a healthy, self-differentiated person.

I return to the woman who anointed Jesus. She did not pay attention to the scolding of the community; she was determined to fulfill her call. She allowed herself to become vulnerable and rejected. One Bible study participant suggested that the woman's actions challenged the authority of the men gathered at Simon's house. The anonymous woman did not ask permission to anoint a guest. She just did what she felt was her duty. At that particular moment, this nameless woman in the Gospel became Jesus' priest. She ministered to him with incredible devotion and compassion. Everyone else was too busy to notice the anxiety Jesus was experiencing. Jesus was in pain; perhaps he was frightened. After all, he was as fully human as you and I are.

The community was far more interested in what this miracle worker could do for them than in who he really was. Did anyone notice he was worried about, and grieving, his own impending death? The answer to this question, it seems, is "no." No one noticed, not even Jesus' disciples. The woman alone was aware. She discerned the miracle worker's need. Her careful attention to the situation is precisely what made her leadership so unique. Are we paying careful attention to the signs around us?

One recurring question asked by the Bible study group was "How did this woman obtain such expensive perfume?" Biblical scholars often suggest that she was a woman of means. Another, more provocative proposition is that she had gathered money from the community. She may have collected it from the many poor and marginalized people who had received so much kindness, healing, and respect from Jesus. She may had concluded that anointing Jesus with perfume purchased with the community's money was the ultimate expression of their love for the one who treated them with dignity. Jesus saw their humanity and not just the faces at the welfare office.

In both stories, the actions of these two courageous leaders can be interpreted as a total surrender to God's will. The task facing Elisha was very complex and risky. Trust in God's guidance and direction was not an option; it was an imperative. The days ahead of the woman were filled with uncertainty and mixed emotions of grief and awe, with experiences of death and resurrection, with times of silence and "good news." Inspired and motivated by the need of the moment and empowered by love, both the anonymous woman and Elisha became instruments of God's extraordinary grace and power.

Act

Act refers to transformation. In this third movement, some level of spiritual, political, and/or social change is expected. It is the movement from reflection into action.

Key questions: What steps do I/we need to take in order to be obedient to the text's invitation? Who needs to be involved? How are we going to implement changes?

Reflections

The stories of Elisha and of the woman who anointed Jesus encouraged the Bible study group to think about *leadership*. In both accounts, we observed two leaders committed to following through with what they understood to be their calls. They both were loyal and faithful, determined to make a difference in the lives of those they touched.

Other themes identified in our conversations were *authority, avoidance, challenge, friendship, transition, succession, grief,* and *mentoring*. One participant asserted, "These texts are so rich in imagery and content. I have never had so much fun studying Scripture while discovering some core values for my ministry. I feel like a child going into a treasure hunt." Indeed, the group played back and forth in significant ways with these two passages. The following is a summary of their conversations, group dynamics, and contributions:

Perhaps the text is inviting us, like the prophets, to stay connected in the appropriate moment, when we might need to rip our cloth of privilege intentionally.

Perhaps we ought to cross our own Jordan Rivers, leaving behind our comfort zones or our worthless battle zones.

Perhaps we, too, are being mentored to enter into a holy struggle.

As some said, "Our battle is against the powers and principalities that consciously inflict pain, suffering, oppression, and annihilation in our world." This battle requires no weapons of mass destruction. It needs, rather, tools of massive *construction*.

Elijah and Elisha were closely followed by other prophets. As leaders, we, too, are carefully watched and follow by our parishioners, co-workers, and sometimes by those in the community that we serve. What we do and say is taken very seriously. For that reason, we must learn not to jump to conclusions, to be honest about our feelings and opinions, and to be wise about when it is appropriate to break our silence. Elisha was asked by his fellow prophets, "Do you know your master is going to be taken by the Lord today?" He did not avoid their question. He shared with them his awareness of the circumstances. He was not ready to express to them how he was feeling and what he was going to do. But he did not push the prophets away. He let them accompany them throughout the entire journey. They, too, witnessed Elijah's departure.

Perhaps, like the woman who anointed Jesus, we need to gather with brothers and sisters who are in tune with the signs of the times. Perhaps we need to enter where we have not been invited, to break open the alabaster jar, and to pour the fragrance of healing and restoration over a friend's head, over a church's heart. "Is God calling us today to break the alabaster jar and pour its contents over our own denomination? Do we need anointing for burial, or for healing?"

Other provocative questions emerged from the group: "Do we need to let this church die so a new one might arise? Or do we work harder toward the eradication of agendas that debilitate and poison the body of Christ?"

Our invitation to holy leadership may imply that we must intentionally rip our individualistic, hidden agendas and create new ones in communion and community. The task at hand for leaders in our era requires open minds with ample space for the development of proactive plans to restore and renew our Christian faith. The matter demands a swift response. This spirit of urgency seems very much like the sense of urgency we witness throughout the pages of Mark's Gospel.

Surrendering ourselves to God's will for our lives is very risky. Doing so, however, is at the top of the list in the job description for holy leadership. It may require that the liberal from the extreme left and the conservative from the extreme right tear down dead-end agendas so that, in the freedom of the spirit of the Anointed One, we all seek reconciliation and resolution. Together, in the spirit of Christ, we can give and receive forgiveness for past ill intentions and then move toward acceptance of our differences. We must be reconciled with one another.

How do we become holy leaders? The answer to this question is not new. As a matter of fact, it has been repeated over and over. For some reason, however, it is often neglected or disregarded. We need to reclaim our ancient, yet timeless, spiritual disciplines. We have become so busy with sophisticated schedules that we hardly find time and space for private and corporate prayer, for fasting, for daily reading of the Scriptures, for simple acts of mercy and charity and justice, for spiritual discernment, and for journaling. These are necessary disciplines that not only inform us but also develop our strengths and empower our lives and communities. These are some of the channels by which we discern God's will for our lives as holy leaders.

Jesus modeled holy leadership for all of us. He prayed for the poor and advocated for them. In the passages we studied, it became important to underscore the response he gave to the complainers: "For you always have the poor with you, and you can show kindness to them whenever you wish" (Mark 14:7). The statement is clear. Jesus is not taking lightly his disciples' responsibility to care for the poor. He also recognizes the inequitable distribution of wealth—a matter that unhappily has yet to be resolved. Thus, Jesus' followers are expected to work toward the creation of just systems in their midst.

Holy leadership always seeks truth and justice. It demands compassion and respect, integrity and humility. I was honored to witness a holy, transforming moment when I joined one of the small study groups. The discussion centered on the women with the alabaster jar. The participants were arguing about lifestyles; and one of the participants said, "I have chosen to break the alabaster jar by claiming who I am." She said this without pretense, claiming her identity as a child of the living God. She felt that her call lay in advocacy.

We cannot dismiss another important lesson about leadership: recognizing that we need to be ministered to. Jesus was the miracle worker, but he also felt bone-tired and drained. He welcomed the gift freely offered to him, the anointing of his body. As leaders, we often feel that we must perform perfectly at all times. One woman in the group said, "Sometimes I am under so much pressure, because people expect so much of me. Would they ask the same things of a white brother? I don't think so." This women recognized that leaders, particularly leaders of color, are frequently exposed in the large fishbowl we call "church." We need to let others minister to us. It is appropriate to say "No, not now," or "I have too much on my plate at this moment." Holy leadership is also about being good stewards of the resources we have been given, including our bodies.

Both the woman with the alabaster jar and Elisha inspired the Bible study group to examine their own leadership styles, their own callings to transform those places where God sends us. The school, the seminary, the denomination, the family, the church, and the community are all places filled with challenges and opportunities to build God's reign in our midst. The incarnation of God's reign seeks holy leadership:

Holy leadership in the new millennium
    confronts the dominion systems of this world,
        allowing those without voice to be heard,
            those without representation to be attended to,
                those without basic human needs to be supplied.

Holy leadership
    summons us to confront the false prophets,
        to denounce the unjust rulers, the indifferent leaders,
            so those without power might find empowerment,
                those without hope may sing a new song,
                    those without dreams
                        may dream great dreams.

Holy leadership
    celebrates Christ's call with humility,
        searches for wisdom and guidance,
            acknowledges its own limitations,
                knows when to pass the mantle.

Where do we stand as leaders today? Do we dare to ask for a double blessing? Are we truly committed to mentoring new leaders, new prophets? Are we ready to pass the mantle? Are we able to recognize and celebrate our gifts? Are we aware of our limitations? Do we need new skills? Do we need to be renewed in order better to serve?

Do we have the courage to break the alabaster jar? Can we handle the pressure, the criticisms, and the rejections? Do we have the stamina to remain healthy and whole? One of the participants said, "I am ready, oh, yes; I am more than ready to break the rules in order to claim my humanity and my leadership." Another said, "I know the transition is not an easy one; I will not fill someone else's shoes. I'll be the leader God wants me to be."

In *The Message*, Eugene Peterson beautifully encourages and validates the call to holy leadership in his translation of 1 Peter 2:9: "But you are the ones chosen by God, chosen for the high calling of priestly work, chosen to be a holy people, God's instruments to do [God's] work and speak out for [God], to tell others of the night–and-day difference made for you—from nothing to something, from rejected to accepted."[10]

We concluded our See—Judge—Act Bible study with an invitation and a prayer.

The Invitation

More than ever, our global village needs holy leadership. Commit yourself to be a holy leader today.

The Prayer

Our beloved God, who is in this place and everywhere,
May your name be blessed in all tongues and dialects.
In our incessant search for wholeness, for courage, and
    for wisdom,
May we work with you to establish a new order of justice,
    of peace, and of love.
Give us a double portion of what we need to become holy
    leaders,
To be willing to enter where we have not been invited
And pour out a blessing for those in grief.
Allow us to bring honor to you and edification to your
    people.

Help us through forgiving others to accept forgiveness.
Strengthen us in the time of testing, that we may resist
   all evil.
For all grace, tenderness and mercy are yours, now and
   forever. Amen.

——➤•➤——

Study Questions

1. How do the images of Latino/Hispanic American experience conveyed here connect with your experience? What surprises you? What excites or encourages you? What troubles you?

2. How does this essay invite you into further exploring multicultural community? What needs to happen for the community in which you live and the faith community of which you are a part to be truly multicultural?

3. What is the meaning of Irizarry-Fernández's "egalitarian quality"? How does this concept affect her understanding of Bible study? How does it impact your understanding of the Bible?

4. How can you envision Ezekiel's vision of the valley of dry bones, or the story of the early church in the Book of Acts, in the light of Latino/Hispanic communities in the U.S.? How does the biblical theme of exile relate with the Latino/Hispanic community?

5. What is your vision of multicultural ministry and community life? How can you bring intentional diversities into your church?

IV. A Critical Feminist Emancipative Reading

―――◆◆――――

Invitation to "Dance" in the Open House of Wisdom

Feminist Study of the Bible

Elisabeth Schüssler Fiorenza

―――◆◆――――

Part I

In the last thirty years or so, feminist biblical studies[1] has been established as a new field of learning with its own publications and methods.[2] It is taught in schools, colleges and universities and is practiced by many scholars in different parts of the world. While feminist biblical studies was not in existence more than thirty years ago, today it is a blooming field of inquiry with many different voices and directions. Hence one would assume that critical feminist study of the Bible is accepted not only as a serious academic field, but also as a method used in preaching and teaching. However, this is often not the case; and various reasons could be adduced to explain the situation.

In the following, I want to proceed in two steps: First, I want to sketch the theoretical ingredients of a critical feminist emancipative hermeneutics. Second, I will outline the interpretive strategies and steps that constitute the critical feminist process of conscientization or coming into consciousness. The second part is hard to sketch on paper, because it requires a process of "doing" and action that is different in every concrete situation of interpretation.[3]

A Critical Feminist Emancipative Interpretation

Because there are so many different articulations of feminism, and many people remain suspicious of the f-word, some preliminary remarks of clarification are necessary.

Preliminary Explanations

First, let me explain how I understand the f-word. My definition of *feminism* is a bumper sticker definition. Years ago, a friend of mine gave me a popular feminist sticker for my car that defines feminism as follows: "Feminism is the radical notion that women are people." This radical democratic definition insists that wo/men are fully entitled and responsible citizens. Hence, feminism should be a common-sense notion in the twenty-first century, rather than a point of controversy. Since this is not the case, it is not surprising that many wo/men still or again do not want to be brushed with the negative label "feminist."

According to this radical democratic definition of feminism, anyone is a feminist who insists that wo/men are not second-class citizens, and who works for the full citizenship of wo/men in society and religion. Politics, not gender, make one a feminist. Men can support the struggles of wo/men for full citizenship; wo/men can be and often are antifeminist insofar as they accept and defend femininity and the feminine as the cultural, religious, and political structure that continues to produce and reinscribe the second-class citizenship of wo/men. The socialization of wo/men into femininity and gendered subject positions shaped and inflected by race, class, and imperial structures produces and internalizes the second class citizenship of wo/men that results in low self-esteem, self-negation, and self-sacrificing relationality.

Second, I need to clarify why I write *wo/men* with a slash. I do so in order to destabilize essentialist understandings of *woman*[4] and to stress the differences among wo/men and within wo/men. I also use wo/men in an inclusive way to refer to disenfranchised men, since marginalized men have been construed in feminine terms. This language usage stands normal "generic" language practice on its head insofar as it asserts that the English word *wo/men* includes men, *s/he* includes he and *fe/male* includes male. This writing of wo/men invites male readers to learn like wo/men to think twice and to ask whether they are meant or not when I speak of the low self-esteem or the great creativity of wo/men. Making conscious and changing ingrained language patterns is an important means of consciousness-raising, since according to Wittgenstein the limits of our language are the limits of our world.

Third, I want to underscore that my own methodological approach is that of a critical feminist interpretation for liberation or emancipation:

- It is *critical* because it understands "text" as rhetorical communication that needs to be evaluated rather than accepted or obeyed;
- It is *feminist* insofar as it focuses on wo/men and their well-being;
- It is liberationist or *emancipatory* because it works with a systemic analysis of the intersecting structures of domination. Since *patriarchy*—which has been and still is used to designate such structures of domination—usually is understood in terms of gender, I have coined the word *kyriarchy*,[5] i.e., *the domination/rule of the emperor, lord, slave-master, father, husband, or elite, propertied, educated man*, as an analytic category to communicate the complex interstructuring of dominations.
- Its goal is not just understanding, but change and transformation. It seeks to change not only the ways the Bible is read and understood, but also to transform wo/men's self-understanding and cultural patterns of dehumanization.

Fourth, although very variegated and theoretically different articulations of feminist biblical studies exist, all of them stress the agency and authority of wo/men to read Scripture differently. Moreover, most of them would agree on the following seven points:

- The Bible is written in androcentric/kyriocentric[6] language;
- The Bible came into being in patriarchal/kyriarchal societies, cultures, and religions;
- The Bible is still proclaimed and taught today in patriarchal/kyriarchal societies and religions;
- Wo/men who until very recently have been excluded from official academic or religious biblical interpretation must be acknowledged as subjects of interpretation;

- Biblical texts and interpretations are rhetorical communications shaped by their socio-political-religious contextualizations;
- If read critically the Bible can be a resource in the struggles for emancipation and liberation.

In short, the objective and goal of a critical feminist biblical interpretation is not just a better understanding of the Bible. Its goal is the *conscientization of biblical interpreters.*

Paradigm Shift

Such a multifaceted, critical feminist interpretation for liberation is positioned within the theoretical paradigm shift engendered by critical theories, liberation theologies, and cultural postcolonial studies.[7] This shift from a modern western malestream to a critical emancipative frame of reference engenders a fourfold change in hermeneutical-rhetorical inquiry:

- a change in interpretive goals;
- a change in epistemology;
- a change in consciousness; and
- a change in central theological questions.

This paradigm shift articulates a change in the aims and goals of biblical interpretation and theology. It begins not with the Bible or biblical history, but with wo/men as hermeneutical subjects and with our experiences of struggle. The task of interpretation is *not just to understand* biblical texts and traditions *but also to change* the death-dealing powers documented by the history of the effects of biblical teachings on the lives of wo/men of all races, nationalities, and creeds. Hence feminist liberation theologies of all colors take as their starting point and as their context of biblical interpretation the experience and voices of those wo/men traditionally excluded from articulating theology and shaping communal life.

Long before postmodern theories, liberationist-feminist theologies have not only recognized the perspectival and contextual nature of knowledge and interpretation but also asserted that biblical interpretation and theology are—knowingly or not—always engaged for or against the marginalized and exploited. Intellectual neutrality is not possible in a neo-colonial, capitalist, and misogynist heterosexist world of exploitation and oppression. It must be noted, however, that it would be a grave misunderstanding to assume that such a liberationist position reinscribes western dualism as some have argued. It does not do so, because it does not assume the innocence and purity of the oppressed. Rather, as the Brazilian educator Paolo Freire pointed out a long time ago, the oppressed have also internalized oppression and are divided in and among themselves.

> The oppressed, having internalized the image of the oppressor and adopted his (*sic*) guidelines, are fearful of freedom. Freedom would require them to eject this image and replace it with autonomy and responsibility. Freedom . . . must be pursued constantly and responsibly.[8]

If both the "oppressed" and their "oppressors" are "manifestations of dehumanization,"[9] then the methodological starting point of a critical feminist interpretation cannot be simply the "commonsense" experience of the oppressed. Rather, all experience, including that of "oppressed" wo/men, must be systemically analyzed and reflected upon. Since wo/men have internalized and are shaped by kyriarchal, i.e., lord, master, father, elite male-dominated, "common sense" mindsets and values, the hermeneutical starting point of feminist interpretation cannot be simply the experience of wo/men. Rather it is wo/men's critically reflected experience of injustice and struggle against kyriarchal dehumanization that must be critically explored in the process of "conscientization."

In short, feminist liberation theologies of all colors[10] derive their lenses of interpretation not from the modern, individualistic understanding of religion and the Bible. Rather, they shift attention to the subjects and the politics of biblical interpretation and its sociopolitical contexts. They claim the hermeneutical privilege of the oppressed and marginalized for reading and evaluating the Bible. In distinction to modern liberal theologies, which address the individualistic questions and ideas of believers facing "nonbelievers," liberation theologies of all colors focus on the experiences and struggles for survival and liberation of the "nobodies" who have been marginalized and dehumanized. Whereas Schleiermacher, the "father of modern hermeneutics," addressed the cultured critics of religion, Gustavo Gutiérrez insists that liberation theologians take up the questions of the "non-persons."[11]

Such an interpretation of the Bible from the sociopolitical positioning of the marginalized and oppressed should not be construed as parochial-confessional and orthodox-doctrinal. Rather, it is to be articulated as ecumenical and political. Its goal is to enable and to defend wo/men's lives that are threatened or destroyed by hunger, destitution, sexual violence, torture, and all kinds of dehumanization. Emancipative biblical interpretations seek to give dignity and value to the life of the nonperson as the presence and image of G*d[12] in our midst. They do not restrict salvation to the soul, but aim to promote the well-being and radical equality of all. Their goal is to inspire biblical readers for engaging in the struggle to transform internalized, cultural-religious kyriocentric mindsets and sociopolitical kyriarchal structures of domination. Feminist liberationists insist that such a reading must take place from the positional perspective of wo/men's struggles for justice and liberation.

Kyriocentric Text and Ideology

A common, popular misunderstanding suggests that feminist biblical interpretation focuses primarily on stories and texts *about "women in the Bible."* Such a misconception overlooks that feminist biblical readings committed to the struggle for changing kyriarchal structures of domination cannot limit themselves simply to *kyriocentric texts about women.* They also cannot identify uncritically with the women characters of the Bible, because these women often represent the kyriocentric values and perspectives of their authors. Rather, feminist liberationist biblical studies seek to underscore the kyriocentric character of all biblical texts and their ideological functions for inculcating and legitimating the kyriarchal order. They seek to adopt methods of interpretation that can demystify kyriocentric scriptural texts and empower wo/men to resist the spiritual authority of the text over their lives.

A critical feminist interpretation pays especially close attention to the function of kyriocentric biblical language that derives its oppressive and its critical revelatory "power" from its cultural-religious contexts.[13] Texts do not have an essential, unchangeable meaning, but they always construct meaning in context. For instance, in a context of emancipatory struggles wo/men may read stories about Jesus without attaching any significance to the maleness of Jesus because they may see the figure of Jesus as struggling against oppression and for liberation. However, reading such stories in a cultural-religious contextualization that places emphasis on the maleness and lordship of G*d[14] and Jesus reinforces wo/men's cultural elite male identification and subordinate subject-location. Such readings shape Christian identity not only as elite male identity, but also as an identity molded by domination and exclusion. This dynamic particularly comes to the fore in the persistent traces of anti-Judaism that pop up even in Christian feminist writings, despite all efforts to eliminate anti-Judaism.[15] Hence, in the act of reading Scripture wo/men suffer not only from the alienating division of self against self and wo/men against wo/men, but also from the realization that being fe/male means never being "a son of God" and being excluded from the divine power of the master/lord/father/husband.

The cultural-religious elite male identification, or kyriarchal "immasculation,"[16] produced by kyriocentric language and culture is never total, however, because of wo/men's conflicting position within at least two contradictory discourses offered by society and biblical religions. Wo/men participate at one and the same time both in the specifically "feminine" cultural discourse of submission, inadequacy, inferiority, dependency, and irrational intuition, *and* in the generic "masculine-human" discourse of subjectivity, self-determination, freedom, justice, and equality. Similarly Christian wo/men participate at one and the same time both in the biblical discourse of subordination and prejudice, *and* in the discipleship of equals. If such a cultural and religious alternative discursive location becomes conscious, it allows the feminist interpreter to become a reader resisting the persuasive power of the kyriocentric biblical text.

When wo/men recognize our contradictory ideological position in a grammatically kyriocentric language system, we can become readers who resist the *lord/master/elite male identification* of the androcentric, racist, heterosexist, classist, and/or colonialist text. If this contradiction is not brought into consciousness, however, it leads to further self-alienation. For change to take place, subordinated people must concretely and explicitly claim as their very own the human values and democratic visions that the kyriocentric text reserves solely for elite, educated, and propertied men.

Insofar as modern "democratic" discourses have been constituted as kyriarchal malestream discourses, the equality, justice, and freedom about which they speak have been only partially realized in religion, society, and culture. Therefore, these partial realizations—which have left their traces in kyriocentric texts—must be reconstructed and imagined differently. Such a reconstructive "imagination" is not pure fantasy. It is historical-religious imagination, because it refers to a reality already partially accomplished in the emancipatory struggles of those who have been subordinated and subjugated throughout the centuries.

Recognizing the kyriocentric dynamics of biblical texts and their functions in wo/men's lives, a critical feminist interpretation is best understood as a rhetorics of inquiry[17] and as a broad interpretative practice which entails epistemological-ideological reflection and sociocultural analysis of power relations. In distinction to a hermeneutic-aesthetic inquiry, which strives for textual understanding, appreciation, application, and consent, a critical-rhetorical feminist inquiry pays attention to the power structures and interests that shape language, text, and understanding. It is concerned not only with exploring the conditions and possibilities of understanding and with appreciating kyriarchal biblical texts, but also with the problem of how one can critically assess and dismantle their power of persuasion in the interest of wo/men's well-being. Therefore, a feminist rhetorical inquiry challenges the dominant model of interpretation, which divides interpretation either into three discrete stages (reading behind the text, reading the text, and reading in front of the text), or separates it into the three discrete operations (explanation, understanding, and application), or constructs a dualistic opposition between so-called "scientific" scholarship and engaged scholarship dedicated to application.

A critical feminist interpretation for liberation argues instead for the integrity and indivisibility of the interpretive process, as well as the primacy of the contemporary starting point of reading. Not only feminist but also malestream biblical interpreters always read in front of the influential cultural classic or religious canonical text. Cultural classics and canonical scriptures, in turn, always already inform our readings. Insofar as they are cultural or religious "classics," they have "performative authority"—a continuing significance and influence in shaping people's thought and life. They function as persuasive rhetorical texts that continue to influence western cultures and biblical religions.

Consequently, a critical feminist interpretation for liberation operates not only with a different understanding of texts, but also with close textual readings that differ from malestream hermeneutics.

Whereas a postmodern reading focuses on the ideologies inscribed in biblical texts and generally rejects a systemic analysis of the multiplicative structures of domination and their impact on texts and readers as "master story," a critical rhetorical analysis of biblical texts remains anchored in just such a systemic analysis of particular historical rhetorical situations and sociopolitical contexts. Hence I continue not only to argue for the possibility of sociohistorical reconstruction, but also to insist on the importance of reclaiming subjugated knowledges as memory and heritage for feminist liberation struggles. Since biblical texts are religious texts articulated in a definite moment of history, their possible meanings are historically, politically, and contextually circumscribed.[18]

In short, the model of critical feminist biblical interpretation, which I have elaborated in *In Memory of Her*[19] and *Bread Not Stone*,[20] theorized in *But She Said*[21] and *Sharing Her Word*,[22] and pedagogically explicated in *Wisdom Ways*[23] is best understood as a practice of rhetorical inquiry engaged in the formation of a critical historical and religious consciousness. Whereas hermeneutical theory seeks to understand and appreciate the meaning of texts, rhetorical interpretation and its theo-ethical interrogation of texts and symbolic worlds pays close attention to the kinds of effects not only biblical discourses, but also biblical readers, produce and how they produce them. Only a complex model of a critical process of feminist interpretation for liberation[24] can overcome the hermeneutical splits between sense and meaning, between explanation and understanding, between critique and consent, between distantiation and empathy, between reading the text "behind" and "in front of" the text,[25] between the present and the past, between interpretation and application, between realism and imagination.

Wo/men's Agency and Authority

The feminist emancipatory tradition of religious agency, justice, and equality for wo/men in which my own work stands has claimed and continues to claim the authority and right of wo/men to interpret experience, tradition, and religion from our own perspectives. This tradition has insisted that equality, freedom, and democracy cannot be realized if wo/men's voices are neither raised nor heard and heeded in the struggle for justice and liberation for everyone regardless of sex, class, race, nationality, or religion.

This feminist tradition of wo/men's religious authority and theological agency remains fragmented and has not always escaped the contextual limitations and prejudicial frameworks of its own time and social location. Nevertheless, its critical knowledge and continuing vibrancy remain crucial for feminist biblical studies. By taking the experience and analysis articulated in feminist struggles to transform kyriarchy as its point of departure,[26] feminist biblical interpretation claims the authority of wo/men struggling for survival and liberation to contest the kyriarchal authority claims and oppressive values encoded in Christian Scriptures. Hence, a critical feminist emancipatory interpretation is akin to the ancient practice of "discerning the spirits" as a deliberative rhetorical spiritual practice.

As theological subjects, feminists must insist on their spiritual authority to assess the oppressive, as well as the liberating, imagination of particular biblical texts. They must do so, I argue, because of the kyriarchal functions of authoritative Scriptural claims that demand obedience and acceptance. By deconstructing the all-encompassing kyriarchal rhetorics and politics of obedience and subordination, critical feminist discourses are able to generate new possibilities for the communicative construction of biblical identities and emancipatory practices.

A critical biblical reading in the ekklesia of wo/men,[27] envisioned as the imaginative space for the radical equality and dignity of every wo/man, understands biblical authority as something that does not require subordination and obedience. It understands truth not as something given once and for all, something hidden and buried that can be unveiled and unearthed in a spiritual reading of biblical texts. Rather, it understands revelation as something ongoing, as fermenting yeast of the empowering presence of Divine Wisdom that can be experienced and articulated only in and through emancipative praxis.

What is "revealed" for the sake of wo/men's salvation, liberation, and well-being cannot be articulated once and for all. The criterion of "wo/men's salvation" is a formal criterion that needs to be "spelled" out in ever new socio-political-religious situations of struggle. It does not inhere in the biblical text, or in the individual subjectivity of the wo/man reader. Rather, it must be articulated again and again within particular historical contexts of struggle.

In short, a critical feminist hermeneutics of liberation does not understand the Bible as an immutable archetype, but as a historical prototype of Christian community and life;[28] the open house of Divine Wisdom without walls and exclusions; nourishing bread rather than engraved tablets of stone. It seeks not only to understand biblical texts and traditions, but also to investigate what they do to those who submit to their world of vision. Kyriarchal biblical values have shaped wo/men's self-understanding and sociocultural political discourses in Western culture. Hence, a critical feminist interpretation for liberation seeks to provide a method of consciousness raising or conscientization that lifts into critical reflection the cultural and religious biblical values and frameworks wo/men have internalized, and to create a pedagogical space for transforming wo/men's self-understanding, self-perception, and self-alienation. By analyzing the Bible's power of persuasion, it intends to engender biblical interpretation as a critical feminist praxis against all forms of domination.

Part II

Beginning the Dance of Interpretation

The process of carrying out a critical feminist biblical interpretation is complex and exhilarating. Feminists have used different rhetorical metaphors and comparisons for naming such an emancipatory process of interpretation: "making visible"; "hearing into speech"; "finding one's voice." I myself have favored metaphors of movement, e.g., turning, walking, way, dance, ocean waves, or struggle. Since Plato attacked rhetoric as "mere cookery," I sometimes have borrowed this metaphor and spoken of biblical rhetorical interpretation as baking bread, mixing and kneading milk, flour, yeast, and raisins into dough, or as cooking a stew, utilizing different herbs and spices to season the potatoes, meats, and carrots that, stirred together, produce a new and different flavor.

The metaphor of the circle dance seems best to express the method of feminist biblical interpretation. Dancing involves body and spirit. It involves feelings and emotions, and it takes us beyond our limits and creates community. Dancing confounds all hierarchical order because it moves in spirals and circles. It makes us feel alive and full of energy, power, and creativity. Moving in spirals and circles, critical feminist biblical interpretation is ongoing; it cannot be done once and for all but must be repeated differently in different situations and from different perspectives. It is exciting because in every new reading of biblical texts a different meaning emerges. By deconstructing the kyriarchal rhetoric and politics of inequality and subordination inscribed in the Bible, feminist interpreters generate ever fresh articulations of radical democratic religious identities and emancipatory practices. Such an emancipatory process of biblical interpretation has as its "doubled" reference point both the interpreter's contemporary presence and the biblical past.

Whether one thinks of the emancipative interpretive process as baking bread, as a hearty "stew," or as a joyful "dance," crucial ingredients, spices, strategies, or moves in a critical process of a multicultural feminist interpretation are:

- experience and recognition of social-ideological location;
- critical analysis of domination (kyriarchy);
- suspicion of kyriocentric texts and frameworks;
- assessment and evaluation in terms of a scale of feminist emancipative values;
- creative imagination and vision;
- re-construction or re-membering;[29] and
- transformative action for change.

These interpretive practices are not to be construed simply as successive, independent methodological steps of inquiry, or as discrete methodological rules or recipes. Rather, they are best understood as interpretive moves and movements, as strategies that interact with each other simultaneously in the process of "struggling for making meaning" out of a particular biblical or any other cultural text in the context of the globalization of inequality. This "dance of interpretation" is taking place on two different levels of interpretation:

- on the level of *biblical texts* and their effective histories of interpretation; and
- on the level of *contemporary interpretations* and *meaning making* in situations of domination and subordination.

Such a critical feminist biblical interpretation continually moves between the present and the past, interpretation and application, realism and imagination. It moves, spirals, turns, and dances in the places found in "the white spaces between the black letters" of Scripture—to use a metaphor of Jewish interpretation.

Hence, it is very difficult to boil down such a dynamic process of interpretation into a logical, consecutive description. If I try to do so here, I hope readers will not see my attempt as a transcript of a process but will use it more like a recipe they need to modify and alter, or as a basic instruction in dance steps they must execute in their own manner in order to keep dancing. We will begin "dancing" by looking at 1 Peter 2:9–3:7 in terms of a feminist rhetorical analysis[30] that presupposes the hermeneutical strategies of a critical feminist interpretation. Then, we will engage the dance steps of a critical feminist interpretation explicitly. In the context of a workshop, groups can engage both levels of interpretation at one and the same time if they have sufficient time and some biblical studies knowledge.

A Feminist Rhetorical Analysis of 1 Peter[31]

The Christian Testament writing called 1 Peter was written at the end of the first century CE and is addressed to "resident aliens" living in the Roman province of Asia Minor. They are portrayed as a marginalized group experiencing harassment and suffering. This pseudonymous epistle is a rhetorical communication in the form of a circular letter between those living in the metropolitan center of imperial Rome, theologically camouflaged as Babylon, and those living in Asia Minor as colonial subjects.

The argument of 1 Peter moves from an elaboration of the theoretically high, but sociopolitically precarious, status of the recipients (1:15—2:10) to the central part of the letter, which addresses the problem of how to behave in a politically correct manner (doing good) with regard to the imperial-colonial authorities, especially if one is a subordinate member of the household (2:11—3:12). The rhetorical strategy then shifts to a more general argument addressing all the intended recipients about "good" behavior in public and the "honorable sufferings" they should expect (3:13—4:11). Finally, the argument climaxes with admonitions regarding the exercise of leadership in the "household of G*d" (4:12—5:11).

Central to the letter's rhetoric is the image of the household (Gk. *oikos*). In the rhetoric of 1 Peter, the Christian community is called "the household of G*d"; and G*d is understood as its Father (*pater familias*) analogous to the Roman emperor. The injunction to subordination is used five times in 1 Peter. Four times it addresses a group of people: everyone in 2:13; household slaves in 2:18; wives in 3:1; and younger people or neophytes in 5:1. Only once is it used in a descriptive praise statement: 3:22 says that angels, authorities, and powers were made subject to Jesus Christ, who "has gone into heaven and is at the right hand of G*d." This last statement makes it clear that the Gk. verb *hypotassein* expresses a relation of ruling and power.

Among others, David Balch's research has documented a growing interest among diverse philosophical directions and schools in the first century to reassert the political ethos of subordination in the household in support of Roman imperial politics.[32] Not only does the injunction to subordination legitimize, but the early Christian apocalyptic language and universe also mythologize the kyriarchal order of the Empire. Like Caesar, Jesus Christ is Lord (Gk. *kyrios*) who is at the "right hand" of G*d, the Almighty. But whereas later times understand church ministry as analogous to Christ's power of ruling, 1 Peter admonishes the elders of the community not to lord it over (Gk. *katakyrieuontes*) those in their charge.

In a rhetorical analysis, the submission-code section in 2:11—3:12 emerges as "the core of the letter"[33] and could be titled, "Become Colonial Subjects/Subalterns." In order to underscore the need for the submissive behavior of household slaves and wives, as well as all Christians, towards the imperial authorities, the author(s) first combines and advocates the imperial ethos spelled out in the discourses about "politics" (*peri politeias* [2:13]) and "about household management" (*peri oikonomias* [2:18—3:7]), then supports it with reference to the example of the suffering Christ and the matriarch, Sarah, and finally moralizes such kyriarchal submission as righteousness and as "doing good" (3:8-12).

The whole section is introduced with an appeal to "honorable conduct" addressed to the "non-citizens and transients" who are hailed as "beloved" (Gk. *agapētoi*). At this point it becomes obvious that the sender theologizes and moralizes the dominant kyriarchal ethos of the Roman Empire and requests that the subordinates realize and live it in their practices of subordination. The rationale and motivation given is missionary: they should conduct themselves "honorably" so that the Gentiles glorify G*d on the day of "visitation" (Gk. *episkopēs*).

The summons to abstain from human desires (Gk. *sarkikōn epithymiōn*) that endanger their lives (Gk. *psychē*) is elaborated and elucidated in vv. 13-17 with the admonition to subject themselves to the emperor as the supreme one and to the governors who are sent by him, i.e., to the imperial administration, so that these recognize them as doing what is right, honorable, or good. The theological justification given here is that such submission, understood as "doing the honorable," is "the will of G*d." Here, the elite masculine ethos of "honorableness" has become "christianized."[34] The overall rhetorical strategy of the letter is summed up in 2:17: Honor everyone, love the "brotherhood," fear G*d, honor the emperor!

The "doing good" of slave wo/men consists in their subjecting themselves even to harsh and unjust masters, so that if unjustly beaten and suffering—if that is G*d's will—they do so for "doing right." Christ's innocent suffering is then elaborated as an example for such honorable behavior in suffering.[35] However, no reference to Christ's resurrection and glory appears.

In a similar fashion, freeborn wo/men are told to subject themselves to their husbands, even to those who are not believers. The goal here is the conversion of their husbands that will be brought about not by their "preaching" to them, but by their proper "lady-like" conduct of purity and subordination as exemplified by the matriarch Sarah, the prime example for female converts to Judaism.

Finally, the "brotherhood" is to be governed not only by mutual love and support, but also by subordination. In 5:3 the "younger" members of the community, who are either younger in age or converts, are told to subject themselves to the older, the presbyters. Although the presbyters are admonished at the same time not to exercise kyriarchal leadership, this injunction still indicates that the argument seeks to fashion the order of the community as one of subordination.

In sum, 1 Peter's Roman colonial rhetoric of subjection advocates the submission of the subaltern migrants and non-citizens in Asia Minor and specifies as problem cases the unjust suffering of slave wo/men and the marriage relationship between freeborn Christian wives and their Gentile husbands. Commentators agree that the context of the letter is one in which Jews and "*Christianoi*" (= "Messianists") were seen as seditious and as a threat to colonial, religious, cultural, and political Roman imperial "customs." The conversion of slave wo/men, freeborn ladies, and younger people in contexts in which the master of the house did not convert constituted already an offence against the "ancestral" laws and customs.

According to Roman laws and customs, the *pater familias*, like the emperor who was called the supreme Father of the empire (Latin *pater patriae*), wielded absolute power over his subordinates in the household and determined the religion of its members. Hence, it was generally accepted as a matter of good civil order that slave wo/men, freeborn wo/men, and all other members of the household practiced the religion of the master and lord of the house. The letter writer is concerned with "honor," construes the "house of G*d" not as temple but as a "household," and advocates submission and the hegemonic ethos of "doing good" so that the recipients will not be attacked as wrong-doers. Hence, he advocates *accommodation* to the kyriarchal order of house and state for missionary purposes as long as such *accommodation* does not interfere with their "Christian" calling.

Because of feminist efforts, most recent scholarship on 1 Peter is aware of the problematic ethical-political meaning and socio-historical effects of the letter's subordination discourse on contemporary society and church. Thus, commentators tend to focus less on the hermeneutical problems posed by the Jewish language of the letter, by the injunction to political subjection, or by the use of the example of Christ to pacify suffering slaves, than on the demand for the subordination of women. In response to feminist interpretation, malestream exegetes feel compelled to write a special hermeneutical excursus,[36] or to articulate special hermeneutical rules for reading texts of submission today,[37] in order to eliminate or mitigate problems modern hearers/readers have with this text.

They also seek to eliminate or mitigate problems by translating the Greek word *hypotassein* with "accept the authority," "defer to," "show respect for," "recognize the proper social order," or "participate in," "be involved with," "be committed to" rather than with "subordinate yourselves." Although such an apologetic translation is primarily concerned with not offending "wo/men" and "liberal" readers/hearers, it conceals the elite male character of subordination which in 1 Peter is "theologized." Such a defensive reading takes the side of the author and his rhetoric of submission, rather than that of those whose subjection he advocates in theological terms.

A critical feminist interpretation in turn reads the text from the perspective of the recipients and takes the side of freeborn and slave wo/men as well as the whole community of resident aliens. The rhetorical tension between the lofty address of the recipients and the ethos of submission which is inscribed in the letter seems to indicate a "rhetorical debate" in the community about what the "will of G*d" demands from Christians living under Roman rule. Slave wo/men, for instance, could have argued that it was "G*d's will" to be treated justly as members of G*d's elect people rather than to suffer patiently the sexual abuse and cross mistreatment at the hands of their masters. Hence, it was justified to run away if their masters treated them harshly. Freeborn well-to-do wives could have argued that it was their Christian calling to proclaim the "good news" to their Gentile husbands, and if they could not convert them to the lifestyle of the elect people of G*d, that it was the "will of G*d" to separate from them by divorcing them. They could have bolstered their argument with reference to Paul who supported the "marriage-free" state of wo/men.

All of the members of the community could have argued that the covenant of G*d demanded that they separate from Gentile society and resist Roman imperial culture because their low-class status as non-citizens and migrants had been changed in and through their conversion. They now were bound together in love and respect and formed a royal priesthood and holy nation, a temple of the Spirit. In consequence, they could not possibly pay obeisance to the Emperor, his governors and other cultural institutional authorities, a political strategy also espoused by the book of Revelation. Thus they could have advocated a separatist stance which would not totally avoid, but might reduce harassment and suffering, since they would not have to mix daily with their Gentile neighbors. Such an interpretation is possible if one reads the arguments of 1 Peter as part of a broad based argument in early Christian communities.

II. The Dance of Interpretation

With this last paragraph we have explicitly begun the hermeneutical dance by engaging in a *hermeneutics of experience* insofar as we have asked what the experience and reaction of the recipients in the first century might have been when they read or heard the author's admonitions. In this hermeneutical step one would also ask questions on the level of *contemporary meaning making*, such as these: what is your experience with this text today? Is it preached or emphasized at certain occasions? How does it reinforce contemporary prejudices? Which statements appeal to you and why? Which do you reject? This hermeneutical step compels us to look at our own experience and reaction when reading 1 Peter 2:9—3:7.

While the oppressive social system of overt slavery is no longer practiced today, the international sex trade is blooming and lucrative. Thousands of wo/men and children are forced or duped into it. Many will feel guilty, fearing the wrath of G*d because of their sinfulness. In a similar fashion millions of wo/men stay in abusive marriage relationships. They blame themselves for provoking violence because they are not obedient and submissive. Christian wo/men readers who have been socialized into a literalist reading of the Bible as the word of G*d therefore understand 1 Peter as telling them that they should accept abuse, suffering, and beatings from their husbands as the will of G*d. When they experience domestic violence and abuse, they blame themselves and accept it as their fault. Many ministers preaching this text underscore that we should suffer just as Christ has suffered. Hence, it is important that feminist Bible study groups and theological education get in touch with such experiences of suffering and abuse and critically reflect on them in terms of a hermeneutics of domination.

A *hermeneutics of domination* analyzes the kyriarchal structures of domination, investigating how they are inscribed in the text by the author and how we reinscribe them in our contemporary readings. In this step one would ask questions on the level of the text, such as these: Does this text reflect Christian and Roman imperial societal values? Is its call to suffering and subordination "the word of G*d," or does it reflect values of the time that reinforce domination and oppression? Here, it is important to show that this text reflects values of Roman imperial domination which the author legitimates with reference to the suffering of Christ when admonishing slave wo/men, and with references to the holy wo/men of the past (Sarah) when admonishing wives.

This hermeneutical step also needs to explore the second level of contemporary meaning making by asking, into what kind of structures of domination and subordination are we socialized today? In order to do so, one needs to become schooled in systemic social-ideological analysis. Bible study groups have to learn how to critically reflect on their social-religious location and ideological context. How are we shaped by our kyriarchal socializations, privileges, and prejudices that inscribe systemic racism, hetero-sexism, class discrimination, and nationalism? How do such socialization, privileges, and prejudices determine our readings of this text? How does 1 Peter function as ideological legitimization today? Both legitimizations of kyriarchal subordination, the christological and the scriptural appeal, are ideological because they justify structures of domination. Hence a hermeneutics of suspicion is called for.

A *hermeneutics of suspicion* is necessary not only because of the kyriarchal structures of domination inscribed in the text and legitimated today by the authority of the Bible. It is also necessary because of the grammatically kyriocentric language of 1 Peter. For instance, in studies about "women in the Bible," usually only the admonitions for wives are understood as speaking about wo/men. Thereby it is overlooked that the admonitions to slaves are also addressed to wo/men, since the term slave includes slave men and wo/men. Hence, the admonition must be read as addressed to slave wo/men since the generic masculine could be used as inclusive. Thus in a "normal" reading of the text that is not aware of kyriocentric language, slave wo/men are erased from historical and contemporary consciousness. Or to give another example from 1 Peter: The community is defined by the masculine term "brotherhood" although the admonition of freeborn wives indicates that women were active members of the community.

Hence, a feminist hermeneutics of suspicion must problematize kyriocentric language on both the level of text and on the level of contemporary meaning-making because it makes marginalized wo/men doubly invisible. For instance, today affirmative-action job advertisements will invite "African Americans, Native Americans, Asian Americans, and women to apply," as if African Americans, Native Americans, Asian Americans are only men and not also women. How one understands kyriocentric language determines one's understanding of early Christianity and of our world today. However, a hermeneutics of suspicion not only scrutinizes language but also lays open the kyriarchal ideological-theological tendencies of the text and of contemporary interpretations. It lays open for critical scrutiny, for instance, the the*logy of suffering that is preached to slave wo/men and inscribed in 1 Peter, or it questions the ethical injunctions to subordination as part of the

kyriarchal ethos of the Roman empire. Hence, it calls for a hermeneutics of evaluation.

A *hermeneutics of evaluation* explores the ideological mecha-
nisms identified by a hermeneutics of suspicion and assesses them
in terms of a feminist scale of values. It asks how much a text
contributes to or diminishes the emancipation and well-being of
every wo/man. Does, for instance, the appeal to the suffering of
Christ contribute to the well-being of slave wo/men to whom it is
addressed? Does the appeal to Sarah's obedience persuade Christian wo/men today to submit to domestic violence? In order to
adjudicate the ethical implications and impact of biblical texts
and their interpretations in the past and in the present, we need a
feminist scale of values and visions. Since the values articulated by
feminists are context- and theory-dependent, they can not be fixed
once and for all but must be discussed and debated. Hence, feminist biblical interpretation can not do its work without the help of
a critical feminist the*logy and ethics. The disciplinary divisions
break down in the "dance" of interpretation. Such a scale of values
and visions can not just be derived from disciplined reasoning but
presupposes the vision of a different world and church. We may
not yet experience the realization of such a different world of well-
being, but it lives in our dreams and hopes that inspire us to continue the struggles for the well-being of all without exception.

A *hermeneutics of creative imagination* seeks to "dream" a world
of justice and well-being different from that of kyriarchal domination. As Toni Morrison so forcefully states in her novel, *Beloved*:

> She did not tell them to clean up their lives or to go and
> sin no more. She did not tell them they were the blessed
> of the earth, its inheriting meek or its glory bound pure.
> She told them that the only grace they could have was the
> grace they could imagine. That if they could not see it,
> they would not have it.[38]

Such an envisioning of an alternative reality is only possible
if we have some experience of it. Hence, wo/men who have not
experienced radical egalitarian love can not imagine it. Wo/men
who have experienced religion only as oppressive and discrimina-
tory but not also as promoting justice and equality cannot imagine
its grace. This insight also applies to the level of text. If we do not
discover visions of equality and well-being inscribed in biblical

texts, we cannot imagine early Christian life and world differently. Hence, it is important to discover the visions of justice, equality, dignity, love, community, and well-being also inscribed in biblical texts, not in order to show that the Bible is liberating or to explain away or to deny the inscriptions of kyriarchal domination in it. Rather we need to do so in order to be able to read the kyriarchal text against the grain.

Feminist interpretation can only imagine a different world of 1 Peter if it focuses on these statements and visions that express a self-identity different from that of domination. Slave wo/men and wives who are told

> you are a chosen race, a royal priesthood, a holy nation, God's own people, in order that you may proclaim the mighty acts of G*d who called you out of darkness into G*d's marvelous light. Once you were not a people, but now you are G*d's people.... (2:9-10)

will have heard this message differently from elite propertied men. Slave wo/men who understood themselves as a royal priesthood and chosen race might have argued that their conversion abolished their slave status; freeborn wo/men might have insisted in the community on their right to "proclaim" the great deeds of the One who had called them, and might have objected to living with husbands who did not heed the call.

Thus a *hermeneutics of historical reconstruction and memory* presupposes and substantiates a hermeneutics of imagination. It uses the tools of historiography to reconstruct the struggles of slaves and wo/men against kyriarchal domination inscribed in early Christian literature in general and 1 Peter in particular. It reconceptualizes and rewrites early Christian history as feminist history and memory. It does so not from the perspective of the historical winners but from the perspective of those who struggled against kyriarchal domination. It does so by placing freeborn wo/men and slave wo/men in the center of its attention. In so doing it changes our image of early Christianity, of church and world today, and of ourselves.

Thus the dance of interpretation culminates in a *hermeneutics of change and transformation.* When seeking future visions and transformations, we can only extrapolate from present experience, which is always already determined by past experience. Hence, we need to analyze the past and the present, biblical texts and our world, in order to articulate creative visions and transcending imaginations for a new humanity, global ecology, and religious community. Yet, I submit, only if we are committed to work for a different future, a more just future, will our imagination be able to transform the past and present limitations of our vision.

To sum up my argument: I have suggested that such a critical rhetorical method and hermeneutical process is best understood as wisdom-practice. Wisdom's spiraling dance of interpretation seeks to serve public theological deliberation and religious transformation. It is not restricted to Christian canonical texts but can be and has been explored successfully by scholars of the traditions and Scriptures of other religions. Moreover, it is not restricted to the biblical scholar as expert reader. Rather, it calls for transformative and engaged biblical interpreters who may or may not be professional readers. It has been used in graduate education, in parish discussions, in college classes, and in work with illiterate wo/men.

The Swiss theologian Regula Strobel sums up her pastoral experience with people who, in parish Bible study groups, have engaged or "danced" this feminist Wisdom-spiral of interpretation. She writes that people who have worked with such a critical multifaceted wisdom process of interpretation have

> changed in an impressive way. In the beginning they still sought the authority of the theologian, who was to decide how a biblical text is correctly understood and interpreted. Increasingly they learnt to understand themselves as subjects not only of biblical readings. On the basis of their experiences they have formulated what was liberatory and what was oppressive. They eschewed the pressure to derive all decisions from the Bible or the attitude of Jesus. For they experienced as meaningful and supportive, as the criterion for decision and action, everything that contributes to the liberation and life in fullness of wo/men and other disadvantaged persons. Thereby they could read even ambiguous Bible texts and be nourished by the liberating aspects without taking over the oppressive ones.[39]

In and through such a critical rhetorical process of interpretation and deliberation, biblical texts such as 1 Peter can be critically investigated and become sites of struggle and conscientization. Patricia Hill Collins has dubbed such a praxis of change and transformation "visionary pragmatism." Feminist visionary pragmatism points to an alternative vision of the world but does not prescribe a fixed goal and end-point for which it then claims universal truth.

In such a process of imaginative pragmatism, one never arrives but always struggles on the way. This process reveals how current actions are part of a larger, meaningful struggle. It demonstrates that ethical and truthful visions of self-affirmation and community cannot be separated from the struggles on their behalf. One takes a stand by constructing new knowledge and new interpretations. While vision can be conjured up in the historical imagination, pragmatic action requires that one remain responsive to the injustices of everyday life. If religion and biblical interpretation are worth anything, they must inspire such visionary pragmatism in the everyday struggles for justice and the well-being of all.

I hope I have been able to give here an impression of how a critical feminist interpretation of Scripture[40] seeks to do the work of Divine Wisdom in ourselves and in the world, bringing about and fomenting radical change, searching for lost and buried emancipatory biblical traditions, and insistently struggling for justice without ever giving up the struggle. In the past decade or so Christian feminists have rediscovered divine Wisdom-Sophia and have made her voice heard among Her people. Through feminist Wisdom-Sophia circles, centers, liturgies, spiritualities, theologies, songs, and Bible study, divine Wisdom-Sophia's wo/men messengers set her table. This table, in the open house of divine Wisdom that has no excluding walls, provides spiritual food and drink in our struggles to transform the kyriarchal structures of church and society that shackle our spirits and stay our hands.

> Wisdom has built her house
> she has set up her seven pillars
> She has slaughtered her beasts
> She has mixed her wine
> she has also set her table
> She has sent out her women messengers
> to call from the highest places in the town. . . .
> Come eat of my bread
> and drink of the wine I have mixed.

Leave foolishness and live
and walk in the way of Wisdom. (Prov. 9:1-6)

Divine Wisdom-Sophia calls Her wo/men servants today from all corners of the earth to search as She does for their lost, submerged, and forgotten liberating heritage, to unfailingly assert the rights of the disenfranchised, and to seek for justice in kyriarchal systems of domination. A critical feminist interpretation seeks to hear Her call and act in the power of divine Wisdom-Spirit, fomenting the radical change that is demanded by G*d's dream of a world of well-being and salvation.

Such spiritual commitments, struggles, and visions for a different Christian self-identity and a world of justice, equality, and well-being do not turn feminists into idealistic dreamers, but gather the *ekklēsia of wo/men* as a movement of those who in the power of Spirit-Wisdom seek to realize the dream and vision of G*d's alternative community, society and world, a dream of justice and well-being for everyone. A Christian theology and biblical interpretation that is feminist is inspired and compelled by Her gospel of liberation and well-being.

———•◆•———

Study Questions

1. How have you experienced texts such as 1 Peter 2:9—3:7? How do you experience them today? How do such texts reinforce contemporary prejudices?

2. Into what structures of domination and subordination are we socialized today? How does our socialization determine the way we read biblical texts?

3. How should we understand the authority of Scriptures when they express kyriarchal values?

4. How do you understand Schüssler Fiorenza's critical feminist approach? What was your experience in using the seven steps or strategies of the "dance of interpretation"? How has your way to interpret Scripture changed?

V. A Critical Relational Reading

A Path Wide Open

Toward a (Critical) Relationship with the Christian Bible

Carter Heyward

Perspective

> How often does the interpretation of the text silence the very wellspring of hope, the desire to speak and to act on behalf of another and of justice?
>
> —Marc H. Ellis[1]

> So when Pilate saw that he could do nothing, but rather that a riot was beginning, he took some water and washed his hands before the crowd, saying, "I am innocent of this man's blood; see to it yourselves." Then the people as a whole answered, "His blood be on us and on our children!" So he released Barabbas for them; and after flogging Jesus, he handed him over to be crucified.
>
> —Matt. 27:24-26[2]

Unless you have been living on another planet, you are aware of the controversy that spun for many months around Mel Gibson's film, *The Passion of the Christ*. One of the major critiques of this movie was that it was anti-Semitic—if not intentionally, then in its likely impact. Having seen the movie twice, my assessment of its anti-Judaism is that it is no more, and possibly even a good bit less, explicitly anti-Semitic than many other Christian portrayals of Jesus' suffering and death. Please be clear that this hardly constitutes a commendation of the film's portrayal of the bloodthirsty religious crowds that insisted Jesus be crucified. It's interesting how often folks defended Gibson's treatment of "the Jews," as well as the endless scourging and crucifixion, by insisting that his film was "true to the Bible."

I have no doubt it *was* true to Mel Gibson's reading of the Bible. And that is the first point I wish to make: there are many ways to read the Bible, many choices of which materials to use and which to omit in our sermons, our classes, our movies, and our daily prayers and meditations. Notice how the lectionaries choose to omit verses and chapters in determining which passages will be read on, say, the second Sunday in Easter. There are also many ways of interpreting the biblical materials we do use—such as choosing to cast a light-skinned, white male as Jesus of Nazareth in a social order that equates lightness and whiteness with goodness and God. Neither Christian Fundamentalists nor the higher critics in the liberal church and academy can claim credibly that there is only one right way to interpret a particular text. In this sense, biblical interpretation is—and always has been—a postmodern adventure.

Let's move on to a somewhat more contentious point: we Christians (and, I would suggest, Jews, Muslims, and other religious practitioners) have a moral obligation either to reinterpret—or, if we cannot reinterpret, to denounce and reject—Scriptural texts that have taken on an oppressive character. Here, I am speaking of biblical passages that have been interpreted as oppressive to one group or another. For example, Mel Gibson agreed, after much pressure from many Christian and Jewish groups, to omit the statement "His blood be on us and on our children" (Matt. 27:25), While he omitted putting any English subtitle to this effect in the film, I am told that the statement (spoken in Aramaic) is indeed in the movie. In the Gospels, "His blood be on us and on our children" occurs only in Matthew and has often been cited to justify the Christian charge that the "Jews are Christ-killers."

Here's what John Dominic Crossan says about this passage:

> This [infamous quotation] is only, repeat only, from the theology of Matthew's community [of Jewish converts to Christianity]. [It is] not from the history of Jesus' execution. The verse means that "the whole people" take

responsibility for Jesus' execution, consider it just, and approve of its implementation. That is why, says Matthew, Jerusalem was destroyed in the year 70 CE (Matthew was written about 85 CE). [Jerusalem] was not [destroyed] because of a very unwise political rebellion (as Mark said), but [as] divine punishment . . . [L]et me repeat—"the whole people" never said any such thing in earlier Roman history but only in later Matthean theology.[3]

Crossan offers a nonoppressive interpretation of a Christian text that has often been used in oppressive, violent, and deadly ways against Jews. The passage has been used so frequently as an anti-Semitic justification that it has become *the* de facto anti-Semitic passage in the Christian Bible. Crossan's interpretation gives Christians "permission" to reject this text as authoritative for Christian life.

But if we did not have Crossan's academic critique of Matt. 27:25, or another biblical scholar's nonoppressive interpretation of this passage, would we claim the authority for ourselves to reject the passage because it has nothing to do with the love of One who "makes justice roll down like waters and righteousness like an ever-flowing stream" (Amos 5:24)? Would we have the audacity, the courage, the bold heart to say, "No, this is not the Word of God; I will not be party to the distortions and debasements of human, creaturely, and divine life that occur whenever the Bible is used to oppress?"

Then Pilate entered the headquarters . . ., summoned Jesus, and asked him, "Are you the King of the Jews?" Jesus answered, "Do you ask this on your own, or did others tell you about me?" Pilate replied, "I am not a Jew, am I? Your own nation and the chief priests have handed you over to me. What have you done?" Jesus answered, "My kingdom is not from this world. If my kingdom were from this world, my followers would be fighting to keep me from being handed over to the Jews . . . ." (John 18:33-36).

This passage is one of many in the Gospel of John that has turned those whom Mark, Matthew, and Luke refer to as "the crowd" (Mark), "crowds" or "people as a whole" (Matthew), or "chief priests and crowds" (Luke) into "the Jews." The Gospel of

John is a favorite book of the Bible for many Christian mystics and poets; I have a special place in my heart for it. It can also be read as the most anti-Semitic book in Christian Scripture. How do we deal with this, we who do not want to lend ourselves, our lives, and our faith tradition to the perpetration of violence against our sisters and brothers? Can we find ways, as Crossan suggests, to understand the Gospel of John in nonoppressive ways by changing its language (referring not to "the Jews" but rather to "the chief priests" or "the crowds")? If we must read John, or if we want to read John in church or any public place, can we commit ourselves to changing its language so that Jesus' antagonists are not identified repeatedly as "the Jews"? I am not a biblical scholar, so unlike Crossan or any number of fine scholars of Scripture, I cannot claim to be a reliable guide in the search for language that is both nonoppressive *and* faithful to the text.

What I do claim to set before you is the theological and ethical urgency for us to say "NO" to use of the Bible as a bludgeon wielded by "good Christians" against people of other spiritual traditions, cultures, tribes, and nations; people of color; poor people; women; gay, lesbian, bisexual, transgender, and omnigender people; people who are older, younger, disabled, or sick; other-than-human creatures and the earth itself. We Christians must reinterpret the Bible, with or without the help of biblical scholars, or we must give it up altogether, at least in those places and ways that hurt human beings, other beings, and the Great Source of all being. We must reject entirely the authority of oppressive Scripture.

> You shall worship the Lord your God, and I will bless your bread and your water; and I will take sickness away from among you.... And I will send the pestilence in front of you, which shall drive out the Hivites, the Canaanites, and the Hittites from before you. . . . Little by little I will drive them out from before you, until you have increased and possess the land. I will set your borders from the Red Sea to the Sea of the Philistines, and from the wilderness to the Euphrates; for I will hand over to you the inhabitants of the land, and you shall drive them out before you (Exod. 23:25, 28, 30-31).

In a discussion of Mel Gibson's film at Episcopal Divinity School in Cambridge, Massachusetts, my colleague Larry Wills, who teaches New Testament and is a convert to Judaism from the Southern Baptist tradition, urged us to realize that just as justice-loving, open-minded Christians have to struggle against the anti-Semitism rooted in the Christian Bible, so, too, God-loving, peace-seeking Jews must resist the exceptionalism present in Jewish scripture, which has too often fueled anti-Palestinian sentiments. Wills was referring to the theme set forth in the passage I just quoted from Exodus, in which the Israelites are told by God to "drive out the inhabitants" of the land because they have been "chosen" by God to "possess" the land. Just as the Gospel of John must be read critically if it is to be read as part of Christian scripture, so, too, should the book of Exodus, with its hostility toward the inhabitants of the land (a hostility encouraged by God), be critiqued by Jews. Marc Ellis, a Jewish theologian of liberation, asks, "And what can Judaism proclaim today? When Jews pronounce the end of humanity in Auschwitz, do they also proclaim it in the prison cells where Hebrew-speaking soldiers torture Palestinian men and women?"[4]

A similar urgency rings in the question of Islamic feminist Irshad Manji when she reflects on the fundamentalist interpretation of the Qur'an by Mohamed Atta (one of the September 11, 2001, hijackers): "What if [he] had been raised on soul searching questions instead of simple certitudes? . . . Maybe he would have stepped back. Maybe. The possibility begs for attention."[5]

A Path Wide Open

In the 1960s and 1970s, progressive Christians in North America were introduced to the "hermeneutic of suspicion," a technique of Latin American liberation theology for reading the Bible critically to understand who is oppressing whom and who has the power to define whose lives. Christians were urged by such liberation theologians as Gustavo Gutiérrez and Juan Luis Segundo to be suspicious of what has come down to us as "orthodoxy"— that is, traditional theological interpretations that serve to hold in place the social, economic, and political status quo. Using a hermeneutic of suspicion, we can critique Christian anti-Judaism in the Christian Bible and Jewish exceptionalism in the Hebrew Bible. Gustavo Gutiérrez spoke of the double task of liberation as "denunciation" and "annunciation"[6]—denouncing and rejecting

oppressive readings of the Bible and announcing new interpretations, much as John Dominic Crossan did in his "announcement"
that the anti-Jewish sentiments in Matthew reflected not God or
Jesus' anti-Semitism but the Jewish Evangelist Matthew's own
mistaken understanding of the destruction of Jerusalem in 70 CE
as God's punishment for the role Jews played in Jesus' suffering
and death.

We must now stretch the boundaries set by liberation theology.
Our work as Christian theologians—and all of us are theologians,
not just the professionals among us—is to denounce oppression, including oppressive biblical texts, to announce liberating
interpretations wherever we can, and to disrupt biblical authority
and shatter its hold over us. For example, womanist theologian
Delores S. Williams pushes further than liberation theologians
like Gutiérrez, Segundo, and black liberation theologian James
Cone. Insisting that the text must always be held accountable to
the particular community—in Williams's case, African-American
women—she argues beyond a theology of liberation, which she
sees as a theology for men, toward a theology of survival against
the odds. Williams develops a survival theology in her work on the
Hagar narrative.[7] Hagar was the slave woman whom Sarah gave
to Abraham when she feared she could not bear him a son. Hagar
became the mother of Ishmael. After Sarah gave birth to Isaac, she
insisted that Abraham send Hagar and Ishmael into the wilderness. Williams contends that though a theology of denunciation
and annunciation may work for oppressed men in racist-capital-
ist patriarchy, oppressed women—poor, marginalized, black, or
otherwise "colored"—must learn to read the Bible not merely as
an exodus manifesto but more basically as a survival resource if
it is to be of any use to them. Delores Williams's insight, which
I echo in my own work, is that Christian women must broaden
our understanding of scripture to include extra-canonical survival
resources—material not in the Bible.

Over the last three decades, many intelligent and deeply moral
white sisters have left the church and its Bible and broken out of
bondage to biblical authority. Many conscientious black Christian
women in the United States have not been as likely to leave the
church. This reflects a historically shaped difference between black
women in the United States, who are generally conscious of their
Christian roots in African-American community, and white North
American women, who often have little sense of communal account-

ability in the context of religion. For white women, as Mary Daly demonstrated in her celebrated exodus from the chapel at Harvard, it is possible to walk away. As a priest and teacher, I have consistently encouraged women to leave the church and even the Bible behind whenever the cost of staying has been their lives—their bodies, their souls, their sense of strength, tenderness, and intelligence, their capacities to love, work, and play.

Thanks to the justice-seeking labors of countless black, white, and culturally and ethnically diverse women, Christian women of many colors and cultures are wrestling with how we can have it all—*ourselves and our faith traditions on our own justice-loving terms*, not simply as individuals but as persons in communities and networks of what feminist theologian Mary E. Hunt has named "justice-loving friends."[8] Can we justice-loving friends read the Bible *despite* its least liberating motifs, such as its patriarchal moorings, as a resource for liberation and healing? What *authority* can justice-loving women and men give the Bible in their lives as Christians?

First and foremost, we need to re-imagine authority itself not as power over and not as that which demands obedience or conformity, but as *a relational resource that grows with us, in the Spirit of mutuality, which is the Spirit of God.*

As a theologian, I can't tell you how humbling it is to be heard well and understood carefully by someone reading your work—to run across someone who may understand you better than you understand yourself. Several years ago, I had such an experience when I read Marc Ellis's *Unholy Alliance: Religion and Atrocity in Our Time*. Someone had recommended it to me as a possible resource for teaching Christology. I had known Marc Ellis only through his work (which I have long appreciated) as a radical Jewish theologian of liberation. Imagine my surprise when I discovered his appreciative use of my understanding of the sacred power in mutual relation to make his own case against the "God of atrocity." Ellis understands the God of atrocity as the patriarchal justification for holding power over one's own people and perpetrating violence against one's enemies.

What Ellis understood in my theology, and what he himself affirms, is that the only way God can be experienced and understood as a source of love, justice, and compassion is *as a path wide open to the future.* Such a God cannot be known primarily, much less only, through dogma, creeds, or the Bible. Ellis insists that God cannot be known "in advance" or through memorials or religious language. God cannot be known or experienced through "a pretense to innocence,"[9] by which Ellis means a self-congratulatory effort to remain pure and spotless, untouched by the sin and evil of the world—a spiritual cut above.

Not until I encountered my theological wrestling through Ellis's interpretation of it did I realize how fully I *do* believe that we humans, together with other creatures, share the sacred work of "creating the possibility of more truth" (Adrienne Rich), "the task of making God exist" (Joan Casañas), "the possibility of swim[ming] with a new stream whose source is still hidden" (Martin Buber).[10] As Ellis writes, much in the spirit of the Islamic feminist Irshad Manji, "Being fully present [in life] has less to do with answers to be dispensed than with a readiness to move within and beyond what is already known."[11]

Being fully present in life means being ready to take a path wide open to God—a path that is an experience of One whom we can meet in our life together on earth as the dimly lit, sometimes altogether hidden, path itself. Along the way, we encounter forces, we are met by surprises, and we are shaken by events that disrupt our lives, shatter our assumptions, and transform, or perhaps obliterate, our experiences and understandings of not only Holy Scripture but also its authority.[12]

No longer are we put under obedience to Jesus, God, Church, or Bible. We have become friends, justice-loving friends, to Jesus, God, Church, and Bible. Together with them we can grow, empowered through the Sacred Spirit of mutuality that is none other than the Holy Spirit, the Christic Spirit. From now on, it is not so much "What does the Bible tell us?" as "What does the Bible call forth in us?" Often, it is both/and—both what we are told and what is called forth in us—yet more radically one than the other: more spirit than letter; more inspiration than doctrine; more mystery than explanation; more what Dorothee Soelle called *phantasy*—a spirited combination of freedom, intuition, and imagination—than obedience to authority.[13]

While teaching my classes at the Episcopal Divinity School, I have become more adamant about presenting a multiplicity of interpretations not only of divine and human/creaturely being but also of how we might best engage the authority of the Bible and other theological resources if we genuinely are committed to the struggles for justice, compassion, and nonviolence. In these classes—one on Christology, the other on Animals, Humans, and the Sacred—it has become clear to me that finding a way to make the Bible fit our spiritual yearnings for connection and compassion is seldom our most creative or faithful spiritual effort. Instead, we should be honest with the Bible, much as we should be with any friend.

Hence, I have found myself confessing that it can be spiritually liberating to realize that on lots of issues and in lots of ways, the Bible is wrong.

> Then God said, "Let us make humankind in our image, according to our likeness; and let them have dominion over the fish of the sea, and over the birds of the air, and over the cattle, and over all the wild animals of the earth, and over every creeping thing that creeps upon the earth" (Genesis 1:26).

The Bible says that humans are to have dominion over the rest of creation, and the Bible is wrong. The Christian Bible, in both Hebrew and Greek Testaments, is too anthropocentric. We cannot interpret "dominion" in a liberating way, any more than we can its derivative, "domination." Only in a spirit of mutuality can we work creatively with the Bible on related themes of creation, humans, animals, earth, and God. We can give and take with the Bible. The Bible gives us something—images of a Creator God who cares about creation—and in turn we give the Bible something—a place in tension with our experiences of the earth and animals as created partners with us, not objects of domination and control. We don't have to give the Bible up or yield our judgments and common sense to it. We can have it both ways: the Bible is a splendid resource book for spiritual journeying and wrestling, and it has its limits, its places of short-sightedness, oversight, ignorance, and oppressiveness.

> Their women exchanged natural intercourse for unnatural, and in the same way also the men, giving up natural intercourse with women, were consumed with passion for one another. Men committed shameless acts with men and received in their own persons the due penalty for their error (Rom. 1:26b-27).

Like many of you, I have been involved in the "gay marriage" debate that continues to be front-and-center news. I have found myself straining for patience in response to liberal Christians who want to use the Bible—a fundamentally patriarchal, hence hetero/sexist, resource—to find justification for same-sex love. There are many spiritual resources queer folks can use to make our case for justice for all. The Bible can indeed be such a resource for justice making, advocacy for the oppressed, and love of neighbor. But the Bible cannot be read honestly as neutral or mute on the subject of homosexuality, any more than it can be read as neutral or mute on the subject of the full participation and leadership of women.

The only way to accept the Bible as a meaningful authority in relation to what the church should teach about homosexuality is to read the Bible *against* itself—for example, as testimony to a God of justice, mercy, and compassion struggling for right relation and liberation, rather than as a rule book written for a sexually proscriptive God, an overseer of patriarchal logic. As bogus as prooftexting is, people on all sides of controversial issues do a lot of it. We lift verses and passages out of context to try to make our points. Intellectually lightweight as this tactic is, it is often spiritually honest. Most Christians "discuss" the Bible by reading or citing favorite verses.

Queer folks can play this game as deftly, and as validly, as those who prooftext to support their homophobia. If we intend to draw upon our friendship with the Bible in our struggles for sexual justice, we can combat biblical homophobia by reading the Bible against itself. For example, we can read Micah 6:8, "What does the Lord require of you, but to do justice, and to love kindness, and to walk humbly with your God?" against Leviticus's condemnations of "abominable" relations between men (Lev. 18:22). Or, we can read Mark 12:30-31, "You shall love the Lord your God with all your heart, and with all your soul, and with all your mind, and with all your strength [and] you shall love your neighbor as yourself. There is no other commandment greater than these," against Paul's exhortation against same-sex love in Rom. 1:26-27. In fact, we can read Paul against Paul. We can read Rom. 8:38-39 and 1 Corinthians 13—in which Paul is a poet of love—against Rom. 1:26-27, in which he is a homophobic vigilante. We can invite the Bible to reject its own authority over us and instead to join us in our wrestling to live responsible, faithful lives in the Spirit of God.

As a lesbian feminist Christian, my gut level response to the hetero/sexism of the Bible has long been "So what?" Regardless of the Bible's messages about lesbians and other women, I intend to lift up and honor my sisters and mothers, my nieces and spiritual daughters, my lovers and friends. It has only been in the last few years, however, that I have been able, along with sisters and brothers throughout the world, to claim the authority to say to the Bible's hetero/sexism, "So what?" and, "We're going to argue about this, because you—the Bible—are wrong about it. When you say what you do about what is natural and unnatural in our sexual relationships, you don't make any more sense than you do when you rave on about the patriarchs and their many wives and concubines having anything to do with God's love in our midst today. Our God loves strong, women-loving women; our sweet woman-loving God keeps opening the path before us."

The Peaceable Kin-dom[14]

When *does* the Bible "make sense" as a source of moral or spiritual authority in our lives? It makes sense when its stories and parables, its poetry and prayers, its histories, mythologies, and theologies illuminate for us the presence of God, a spiritual power moving in history, molding our lives, collectively and individually, in the shape of justice-love, compassion, and reconciliation. When functioning most creatively, the Bible's words transcend the specifics of the times and places in which it was written; we are able to read it, hear it, think about it, and wrestle with it as the Word of God for us today. This kind of dynamic relationship with the Bible enables us to experience it as a resource of spiritual authority—not because we accept all of its words as "right," since we do not, but because we are *involved* with the Bible, much as with a friend or co-worker, a spouse or lover, a parent or child, a teacher or student, with whom we struggle to discover the truth that empowers us to do our best.

> The wolf shall live with the lamb,
> The leopard shall lie down with the kid,
> The calf and the lion and the fatling together,
> And a little child shall lead them.
> The cow and the bear shall graze,
> Their young shall lie down together;
> And the lion shall eat straw like the ox.
> The nursing child shall play over the hole of the asp,

And the weaned child shall put its hand on the adder's den.
They will not hurt or destroy on all my holy mountain;
For the earth will be full of the knowledge of [God]
As the waters cover the sea (Isa. 11:6-9).

How might we understand Isaiah's vision of the "peaceable
kin-dom" of God? Can it be prophetic? Does it convey some
truth? Do we, and how, believe that this passage is the Word of
God? Can we believe this in relation to historical relationships of
animosity and violence between peoples, cultures, and religions or
in relation to the earth creatures that graze and lie down together
in Isaiah's vision? Historically, can we imagine the day when the
victors and vanquished, the oppressors and oppressed, the haves
and have-nots will live in peace: When the Hutus and Tutsis no
longer wage violence against each other in Rwanda? When Osama
bin Laden and George W. Bush and their respective followers no
longer represent predator and prey? When Martin Luther King
Jr.'s dream of a just society in which little black children and little
white children can live together becomes simply the way it is?
What is Isaiah trying to say to us about this vision, this eschato-
logical scenario, that may seem so unreal to us?

The prophet is telling the people of Israel and, through them,
us that it is not unreal to imagine a peaceable realm in which God's
people and creatures live together, managing our conflicts and
tensions peaceably rather than violently. The path wide open to
this sacred realm—both here and not here, present in intimations
and glimpses, yet always coming, never fully arriving—is a path of
mutuality, a path of right relation in which we learn together how
to confess our complicities in systems of evil and destruction that
rain down death upon God's people and creatures. Together, we
learn how to confess our sin and to go and sin no more—things
we can do only partially and only with one another's encouragement and prayer. We learn how to forgive others, even as we need
others to forgive us. This is how God works, drawing each and
all of us together in her Spirit of mutual contrition and forgiveness. Whenever and wherever there are oppressed persons, violated creatures, victims of violence and injustice, these sisters and
brothers—the least among us—will lead us to the path wide open.
Without guides from those who are outcast and marginalized, we
cannot find the path. This is what sacred history is all about: sharing a sacred path to the peaceable kin-dom, a path wide open to

which we are led, morning by morning and day by day, generation upon generation, by the least of these, our brothers and sisters, with names and faces and cultures and languages and religions that differ from our own.

Of the so-called "natural" realm of earth and animals, eco-feminist process theologian Jay B. McDaniel has this to say:

> Not all of us will assent to the specifics of Isaiah's vision [of the peaceable kin-dom]. It is difficult for us to imagine an end to predator-prey relationships. Still, we can rightly share that empathy for life which stimulated the author to articulate the vision in the first place. Behind that empathy we can indeed discern divine inspiration.[15]

Indeed.

I have just finished writing a small book in which I introduce horses as spiritual teachers.[16] I share some of that book with you here to place Isaiah's vision in the context of creation itself—a setting for our ongoing struggle in God, by God's power, for more fully mutual relations between and among all of us. Whether or not I am being true to the Bible, and the Bible is being true to me in this study are questions whose answers will become clearer over time. Living in the Spirit, including our living relationships with the Bible, will always require "revolutionary patience" (Dorothee Soelle), because we seldom know in advance whether we are living, speaking, writing, or acting faithfully.

Here is an excerpt from my book, *Flying Changes*:

> I cannot deny what I am hearing. Against the terrible backdrop of war . . . , the Spirit is yearning, as ever, to be born among us, urging us toward opening more fully to her presence and her needs. No stranger to fear and terror, conflict and tension, violence and killing, she nonetheless generates peace, always peace. She also brings death as well as life. Fear as well as comfort. The animals and other creaturekind can help us see that we Christians seldom have encouraged one another to experience fear and, at some point, even death not as bad or as punishment but rather as dimensions of life in the realm of the Spirit. To be sure, our fear of difference, otherness, and

unknownness can, and often does, function demonically in our lives, leading us into evil. In these cases, death too often is a consequence of injustice, oppression, evil. But neither fear as an emotion, nor death as a passage beyond life as we know it, is in itself wrong or ungodly. The rest of creaturekind may embody these dimensions of our shared life in God [and] help us realize that it's okay to be afraid and even, at some point, to die; and that through fear and someday death we will come face to face with the Sacred in her great wisdom.[17]

What follows is an image of the peaceable kin-dom from *Flying Changes*:

On January 11, 2002, Sister Angela (a 75-year-old Poor Clare nun—also one of the first Anglican women priests in Australia—headed out with me on foot toward the stables, which were about a half mile from home. . . . The weather was perfect, one of those unseasonable January days in the South when riding outside is not only possible but glorious, in an arena infused by the stillness and silence of winter filtering through trees that are bare. Sitting there in jeans and a sweatshirt, I watched from the bleachers as Angela and the quarter horse Red began their ride.

The first thing I noticed was how happy both of them seemed. Angela was beaming and Red, in her own horse-way, was letting us know that she too was feeling fine—ears forward and at ease, head and neck relaxed, mouth and tongue indicating a willing connection with Angela, legs and body moving softly and rhythmically under Angela, whose own movements were barely perceptible. . . .

I'm not enough of an equestrian to describe in detail what I saw, but I can tell you that Red was moving in such a way that her body seemed to be floating. There was not a hint of heaviness or awkwardness, and Angela's embodied energy seemed to reflect Red's elegance. Theologically, I'd say they were generating this energy together, and that it was sacred.

Then and there I realized that Angela and Red were becoming one living, moving body. . . . Thirty or forty minutes passed. . . . Whatever the Spirit might have been "telling" Angela and Red, I was being shown by the two of them and the Spirit between them something I had never realized before in quite this way: God really does make us one. We really are one in the Spirit and this does not negate or diminish our otherness or separateness or diversity. Angela was not becoming a horse and Red will never be human and yet, together, with one another's help, each was transcending the limits of species and particularity to become more than either could be by herself. . . .

It is how we achieve our balance—as humans, as creatures, all of us shaped by a power that moves through us toward greater mutuality. And the balance we achieve in such powerful relational moments is between our separateness and our unity, our diversity and our commonality. God lives among us most fully in the spaces between us, where sacred power is generated. To ride, to love, to work, to live in these spaces is to live "in the balance" that is at the very core of God.[18]

As I was finishing the first section of this essay, I watched for the third time a delightful movie that always helps me love God—*Babe*, which to me is a little piece of holy scripture: "The pig and the farmer regarded one another, and for a brief moment, something passed between them."

"Regarding one another," we share a path wide open, and something passes between us. Only insofar as the Christian Bible (and other holy scripture) empowers us to share this path does it speak to us with truly spiritual authority. When this happens, we do indeed hear the Word of God, and it is good!

Reading Scripture Boldly

During our session of the Anna Howard Shaw Center's "A Mosaic of Voices" Bible study series, the small Bible study group listened to my presentation, "The peaceable kin-dom." Afterward, we discussed the presentation for about an hour, focusing on how pastors and lay leaders might teach critical Biblical studies at the parish level, where some folks often seem not to want to think critically about the Bible. Three ideas energizing the group of eight women were biblical authority, individual relationships with the Bible (all of them significant but not necessarily friendly), and the role that stories can play in teaching people how to think critically about anything, especially—for many Christians—the Bible.

On Biblical Authority

I began the Bible study with a quote from my book *Touching Our Strength*:

> Genuinely creative authority, sacred at its root, is in our hands. It moves us more fully into our bodyselves-in-relation. It touches and often frightens us as it calls us forth to become more fully who we are already: interdependent and mutual participants in this journey we call life . . . . In this spirit, I [define] authority as that which calls into being "something" that is already and, for that reason, can be trusted. The reason we can trust the authority of the story or resource or person is that it does not impose an extraneous set of expectations upon us but rather evokes "something" we already know, or have, or are. We need authority precisely for the purpose of helping us discover, recover, empower, and encourage ourselves and one another.[19]

One woman responded that she brings the authority of having experienced being a mother to her understanding of the Bible. Another spoke of the authority of having a good, critical theological education. As participants shared, they were able to name many of the sources of authority in their lives that they bring to Bible study. These sources include traditional Christian teachings about God's acting in history, the power of Jesus' witness, the centrality of forgiveness to Jesus' life and work, the spiritual challenges of other religious traditions, and important books, films, music, art—resources seasoned through folks' own life experiences as parents, lovers, siblings, children, justice workers, peace activists, animal lovers, artists, environmentalists.

One of the most interesting and valuable insights offered during this discussion was that *people bring authority to Bible study only insofar as they let themselves realize their own authority*. For this reason, a major pastoral and educational role for a parish minister, lay or ordained, is to help people realize and claim the authority of their own experience. The group agreed that for them, the Bible carries a huge amount of negative baggage, as well as positive value; deconstructing its damaging, debilitating weight is a critical and creative task Christian leaders share.

On Our Relationships with the Bible

To further the consideration of biblical authority, I asked participants to imagine *themselves*, each of them, in *intimate relationship* with the Bible—a personal relationship as with a life partner, a business partner, a best friend, an estranged partner, or even an enemy. I asked them to consider to what extent this relationship would carry any authority in their lives, and how they might describe this authority. For most participants, their relationship with the Bible felt similar to a relationship with an estranged spouse, a former lover, or—in one case—an old, almost-but-not-quite-forgotten friend. No one experienced her or his relationship with the Bible as a simple thing. For each person, this particular relationship was complex, fraught with ambivalence, and, in most instances, strong emotion. One workshop member exclaimed, "Well, of course, every serious relationship has its ups and downs!" One rejoined: "Yes, how often intimacy has a love-hate edge!"

Several participants said that for the first time, they were beginning to realize that it's really okay to hate much about how the Bible is used and abused, as well as to love much of what we encounter in its pages, images, stories, and spiritual and cultural traditions. Our relationships with the Bible are ongoing, relational journeys that will remain complex sources of creative inspiration *and* of damaging memories and impact—both/and. Thinking about Biblical authority as a complex relational journey sparked considerable enthusiasm and commended itself as a likely resource for ministry in parishes and other pastoral and educational contexts.

As Christian theologians, one of our tasks along the journey is to understand "scripture" as a broader resource than the Bible itself. Recalling the contributions of womanist theologians Katie G. Cannon and Delores S. Williams to our discussion,[20] I reminded the participants that many womanist and feminist theologians have long since moved beyond the assumption that the Christian Bible is the only sacred scripture from which Christians can or should draw. "The sources and resources of our spiritual authority—our scripture—[must] be open, with us, to change and surprise."[21]

Thinking Against the Text

It is not hard to read the Bible against itself, because the Bible is filled with contradictory dicta. A similar method used by Christians who have a complex, critical relationship with the Bible is to "preach against the text." This is something all Christians can be encouraged and helped to do in this Bible study. This process entails resisting the assumption that simply because the "Bible says so"—that is, because the particular English translation we happen to be reading "says so"—what we are reading is God's word, expressive of God's will. Just as Jesus took it upon himself to argue with and re-image the scripture of rabbinic Judaism, so too we are urged by the same Spirit of God to wrestle with, and think against, the biblical text whenever it contravenes Micah's call to do what is just, love what is merciful, and walk humbly with our God (Micah 6:8).

The group then divided into three subgroups. Each subgroup selected a passage and planned a presentation on that text for the entire group. Each group considered these questions:

1. With what authority does your group speak?
2. What is your group's understanding of biblical authority?
3. Suppose a church school group has asked you about this passage: what issues or questions would you need to explore in order to respond?

The three groups' participants affirmed their own experience as foundational to the authority of the groups—their experience as relational persons, their group experience as persons in relation to each other, each person's relation to the Christian church, including the Bible. Each individual and all three groups had a variety of experiences of biblical authority—some more positive, others more negative—but everyone was excited by the prospect of understanding biblical authority in more relational ways.

The first subgroup considered Matt. 27:24-26:

So when Pilate saw that he could do nothing, but rather that a riot was beginning, he took some water and washed his hands before the crowd, saying, "I am innocent of this man's blood; see to it yourselves." Then the people as a whole answered, "His blood be on us and on our children!" So he released Barabbas for them; and after flogging Jesus, he handed him over to be crucified.

Historic issues in this passage include the relationship of Pilate and the Roman government to the Jews in the Roman Empire and, in particular, to Jewish religious leaders; Pilate's role and responsibility for Jesus' death; the Jewish religious leaders' role in relation to Jesus' death. Another historic issue is the audience for and purpose of Matthew's Gospel. What was Matthew's relation to the Jewish Christian community? What did Matthew mean when he put the words "His blood be on us and on our children!" in the mouths of "the [Jewish] people as a whole"? A primary pastoral and moral issue raised by the group is the prevalence of Christian anti-Judaism and anti-Semitism fueled by this passage. I suggested that the historical problem must be addressed by ethically responsible Christian leaders. Scholars such as John Dominic Crossan, Elisabeth Schüssler Fiorenza, and Richard Horsley provide helpful resources for studies of the anti-Judaism in Christian Scriptures.

The second group examined the creation narrative in Gen. 2:26:

Then God said, "Let us make humankind in our image, according to our likeness; and let them have dominion over the fish of the sea, and over the birds of the air, and over the cattle, and over all the wild animals of the earth, and over every creeping thing that creeps upon the earth."

Participants noted that the primary theological and ethical issue here, both historical and contemporary, concerns the relationship of humankind to the rest of creation, a relationship usually viewed as one of domination and utility, of exploitation. The groups had a lively discussion of the following questions: Can a relationship of domination ever be a "right relationship"? Is it mere fantasy to imagine mutuality between humankind and the rest of creation? What might such mutual relation—if it is right, good, desirable, possible—involve? What other parts of the Bible—Hebrew or Greek testaments—can be used to clarify, sharpen, or preach against this text? What other "scripture" from the works of such environmentalists and eco-theologians as Rachel Carson, Jonathan Schell, Carol Adams, Jay McDaniel, Daniel Spencer, Larry Rasmussen, and Rosemary Radford Ruether can be drawn upon to clarify, sharpen, or teach against a theo-ethic of control and domination?

The third subgroup studied an excerpt from Paul's letter to the people of Rome:

> Their women exchanged natural intercourse for unnatural, and in the same way also the men, giving up natural intercourse with women, were consumed with passion for one another. Men committed shameless acts with men and received in their own persons the due penalty for their error (Rom. 1:26b-27).

For the remainder of the session, the discussion focused on the fact that, historically, the Roman Empire and the early Christian church, like Judaism, were patriarchal and that patriarchy *requires* sexist and heterosexist ordering of gender relations. We talked about what this sexism and heterosexism actually involves. The male must be "on top," politically, spiritually, socially, and sexually. It's only "natural"—right and holy. There can be no doubt that in ancient Israel, and many centuries later in Rome, "homosexual" activity was viewed as despicable. Today, however, we possess a great deal more scientific understanding of the world, society, and human beings—including matters of gender and sexuality. What is required *now*, theologically and ethically, to create right relations between and among people of different or similar gender-identities? How do our experiences and understandings of biblical authority contribute to our understanding of this text? How can our understandings of "sacred text" be expanded through other resources, such as the work of Bernadette Brooten, Kelly Brown Douglas, Marvin M. Ellison, and Virginia Ramey Mollenkott, to name only a few sisters and brothers who have wrestled at the intersections of gender and the Bible? The Bible study ended with a good deal of excitement about taking these learnings out into the parishes and other church communities.

————◆————

Study Questions

1. How do you respond to Heyward's suggestions regarding arguing with the Bible, or reading "against" the Bible, or reading the Bible against itself?

2. What sense of your own authority, and of that of your group or community, do you bring to the interpretation of a biblical text?

3. How do you and your community respond to the heterosexism of the Bible? What do you think is required now, theologically and ethically, to create right relationships among people of different or similar gender-identities? How might your own experience and understanding of biblical authority contribute to that work, or serve as an impediment to it?

4. What other resources do you bring to the interpretation of the biblical text; what other resources do you feel you or your community lack in order to interpret the Bible in a life-giving way?

5. How have you spoken, or do you now speak, "against the text" as you engage it in your own life and work? How might a critical relational approach to the Bible be put into practice in your faith community?

Conclusion

Katheryn Pfisterer Darr

As I write this conclusion, I imagine you, our readers, as a diverse group of women and men representing a broad spectrum of races, cultures, ethnicities, social locations, ages, sexual orientations, educational backgrounds, and religious traditions. Each of you has devoted time and reflection to this book. And we—the contributors, editors, and publisher—gratefully acknowledge your participation in our joint project.

Though the printed words on each page of every copy of *Engaging the Bible* are the same, I am aware that no two of you have read precisely the same book! This is because the meaning of any literary work depends not only upon what the *text* brings to its readers, but also upon what *readers* bring to the text. There can be no purely "neutral" or "objective" reading, because all readers are, to a significant degree, products of their times, contexts, experiences, beliefs, and imaginations.

Two simple examples illustrate this observation. First, most of us have read a novel and subsequently watched a movie based on that novel. Viewing the film, we may be surprised, even disgruntled, because its characters look so different from how we had imagined them. Second, most of us have read critical reviews of books, poems, or plays, and been amazed that the critic's impressions and interpretations could be so alien to our own. How, we ask, can people construe the same work in such diverse ways? In both cases, the answer resides, in good measure, in the fact that our interactions with texts (or films, or paintings, etc.) are invariably conditioned to some extent by the presuppositions, ideas, and judgments that shape our own, unique worldviews. By the same token, no author, film director, or artist creates *ex nihilo* ("out of nothing") since they, too, are products of their times, contexts, experiences, beliefs, and imaginations.

Given our diversity as individual readers and communities of readers, I can imagine that readers of *Engaging the Bible* have received, interpreted, and assessed its essays in myriad ways. On one hand, persons who have always approached the Bible as the literal "Word of God" might be startled when Carter Heyward asks, "Would we have the audacity, the courage, the bold heart to

127

say, 'No, this is not the Word of God; I will not be party to the distortions and debasements . . . that occur whenever the Bible is used to oppress'?" Those who accord ultimate authority to Scripture might be shocked by Elisabeth Schüssler Fiorenza's description of biblical texts as "rhetorical communication that needs to be evaluated rather than accepted or obeyed." Women and men who have esteemed Rahab as a biblical heroine, and celebrated that (even) a Canaanite woman could be depicted "positively" within a literary corpus riddled with anti-Canaanite propaganda, might resist when invited, through Kwok Pui-lan's eyes, to judge her portrayal negatively as "a representative of the 'good native' who acquiesces voluntarily to the conquerors, offering them protection and assistance in subduing her own people." And persons who have read the Bible not only as *descriptive* of its ancient social, political, and religious contexts, but also as in some sense *prescriptive* for contemporary cultures and societies, might be taken aback by notions that "kyriocentric" biblical texts "inculcate" and "legitimate" oppressive structures, that "biblical interpretation and theology are—knowingly or not—always engaged for or against the marginalized and exploited" (Schüssler Fiorenza), and that they should reckon with the possibility that "on lots of issues and in lots of ways, the Bible is wrong" (Heyward). "Is it not more likely," some readers might ask, "that the fault lies not with the biblical texts, but with their interpreters?"

On the other hand, even readers steeped in the theories, methods, and hermeneutical strategies of Latin American, feminist, African-American, and postcolonial scholarship might wish to challenge at least some of our authors' presuppositions and judgments. What, they might ask, does it mean when Carter Heyward states that Christians "have a moral obligation to reinterpret—or, if we cannot reinterpret, to denounce and reject—Scriptural texts that have taken on an oppressive character"? How, and to what extent, can we reinterpret such texts? What does rejecting them mean? Should we excise them from our canons? Should we simply ignore them? Or should we remain in dialogue with troubling texts, acknowledging that their contents are unacceptable, but maintaining nonetheless that the dialogue is important and should not be avoided? And while some readers might criticize Aida Irizarry-Fernández's and Cheryl Townsend Gilkes' essays because they say little about how the Bible has been used to marginalize/oppress Latinos, African-Americans, etc., still others might question why, in light of their negative critiques, Heyward and Schüssler Fiorenza continue to expend their intellectual gifts, energy, and time interpreting Scripture. If the Bible—a classic in Western culture—and its long history of interpretation are patriarchal and oppressive, yet continue to wield "performative authority" (Schüssler Fiorenza), can we realistically hope to transform deeply-ingrained "cultural patterns of dehumanization" to any significant degree?

I raise these comments and questions to illustrate how you, as readers, might or might not have responded to the preceding essays. I also recognize that some of you may have begun *Engaging the Bible* from one place, only to discover that your ideas and understandings have changed over the course of your reading. In what follows, I shall identify and comment upon five important, recurring themes in this volume. My hope is that further reflection upon these and other themes will enrich your own engagements with the Bible.

1. We have identified texts, including biblical texts, as products of their social, religious, and political contexts. Like modern-day writers and readers, the biblical authors and redactors neither lived nor worked within a vacuum. They too were products of their times, experiences, and beliefs. In some cases, they expressed what still strike us as immutable truths ("love your neighbor as yourself"). In other instances, however, they reveal—even champion—presuppositions and judgments about, e.g., institutionalized slavery (which is sometimes regulated, but nowhere flatly condemned in either the Hebrew Bible or the New Testament), gender (where, e.g., women are placed firmly under the control of male family members and denied equal legal standing), and divine justice (where, e.g., human suffering is attributed to divine displeasure and retribution) that we might well deem unacceptable.

2. We have highlighted the strategic, rhetorical nature of biblical literature, challenging contemporary readers not only to recognize and reject its attempts to align audiences' worldviews with its own, oppressive points of view, but also to adjudicate among the diverse, often conflicting perspectives it advances. No less than contemporary authors, different creators of our biblical literature believed, supported, and defended a diverse array of theological, political, and social viewpoints; and in their writings, they sought to persuade their audiences to perceive "reality"—including divine reality—in their way, rather than in some other way. As readers, we ought to claim

the authority to scrutinize and evaluate these rhetorical strategies, as well as those of generations of their interpreters, in order to assess whether or not to be persuaded by them.

3. In light of these two observations, we have both challenged notions that the Bible contains the utterly authoritative, immutable, unquestionable, and sufficient "Word of God," and redefined divine revelation as an ongoing process that invites our participation, as "each generation of Christians brings new questions, as well as its own insights, in comprehending God's continuous revelation in history, to the text" (Kwok Pui-lan). In some cases, we are compelled flatly to declare to biblical texts, "No, in this I cannot follow you." At other times, we are able to wrestle "splendid resource[s]" for "spiritual journeying and wrestling" from its pages, despite "its places of short sight, oversight, ignorance, and oppressiveness," to "invite the Bible to reject its own authority over us and instead to join us in our wrestling to live responsible, faithful lives in the Spirit of God" (Heyward). On still other occasions, we will delight in the discovery that the Bible "illuminates for us the presence of God, . . . molding our lives . . . in the shape of justice-love, compassion, and reconciliation" (Heyward). Aida Irizarry-Fernández's essay, in which she fruitfully applies the See-Judge-Act method of biblical inquiry to several biblical texts, illustrates just how delight-filled that discovery process can be.

4. The task of interpretation places upon us a responsibility actively to respond to God's mandate on behalf of poor and oppressed persons and communities around the globe. In her essay, for example, Cheryl Townsend Gilkes lifts up how Africans and their African-American descendants engaged the King James Version of the Bible with "a critical vision shaped through their experience as slaves and their observations of the Christianity of the white people who enslaved them and supported their enslavement." Their "prophetic-apocalyptic reading of the English Bible" emphasizes the prophetic call for "justice, mercy, liberation, and human equality" on one hand, and the apocalyptic affirmation of a God "who requires answers from us about our participation in the prophetic dimension" on the other. Addressing Christians in the United States, Gilkes spells out some of the social inequities around and before us, reminding her readers that the Gospel requires more than study and lip service: it also lays claim on how we live our lives:

Christians in the United States face not only the inequities of race, ethnicity, sexual orientation, gender, and
physical abilities but poverty, which leaves thousands of
people dying daily of HIV/AIDS and other preventable
illnesses. These people are laid at the gates of a nation
where many have defined morality as a political issue.
If we hear Moses and the prophets, then we know that
our relationship with those who are poor, hungry, naked,
bound, and sick (Matt. 25:31-46) will be interrogated.
If we cannot give an account that places us on the right
hand of the King, then it will not matter that Jesus was
crucified and rose from the dead.

5. Finally, all of the essays in *Engaging the Bible* remind readers that—despite its potential power to oppress, to distort, and to
exclude—the Bible still can be a resource for "visions of justice,
equality, dignity, love, community, and well-being" (Schüssler
Fiorenza). Its words still can "transcend the specifics of the times
and places in which it was written." And it still can be a resource
"if we genuinely are committed to the struggles for justice, compassion, and nonviolence" (Heyward). Those women and men who
have rejected the Bible altogether because the pain it summons in
them is too great to bear deserve our understanding and respect.
But for those of us who—like Jacob at the Jabbok River—wrestle
with their Scriptural traditions, knowing they will be wounded,
but demanding a blessing nonetheless (Gen 32:25-27), both the
Hebrew Bible and the New Testament remain among our most
engaging conversation partners. We read them *listening* for the
Word of God.

Notes

I. A Prophetic Apocalyptic Reading

1. James Baldwin, *The Fire Next Time* (New York: Bantam, 1963), 141.

2. C. Eric Lincoln and Lawrence Mamiya, *The Black Church in the African American Experience* (Durham, N.C.: Duke University Press, 1990), 388-91.

3. The text used for the purpose of this paper is the version of the spiritual found in James Weldon Johnson and J. Rosamond Johnson, *The Books of American Negro Spirituals* (New York: Viking, 1969), 11.

4. Ibid., 96.

5. I am grateful to the Nigerian critic, Chinweizu, for the term *orature* as a tool for exploring oral tradition.

6. Henry Louis Gates, *The Signifying Monkey: A Theory of Afro-American Literary Criticism* (New York: Oxford University Press, 1988), 127ff.

7. Whenever I speak of *dimension*, I am using Ninian Smart's approach to exploring religious worldviews. That approach examines six dimensions: the experiential; the mythic; the doctrinal; the ethical; the ritual; and the social dimensions. Ninian Smart, *Worldviews: Crosscultural Explorations of Human Beliefs* (New York: Simon and Schuster, 1983).

8. Mary Warnock, *Imagination* (Berkeley: University of California Press, 1976).

9. Thomas L. Webber, *Deep Like the Rivers: Education in the Slave Quarter Community, 1831–1865* (New York: W.W. Norton, 1978), 80–90.

10. "Po' Lazarus" also shows up in a secular work song in which Lazarus is the unjust victim of a violent southern sheriff. The work song, a version of which was recorded at Parchman Prison by Alan Lomax in 1959, places Lazarus within the oppressive matrix of sharecropping and debt peonage; he is killed because he resists being a victim and his body is displayed in such a way for all to see his "wounded side." This version is part of the soundtrack for the film *O Brother, Where Art Thou? See Soundtrack: O Brother, Where Art Thou?* (Universal City, Calif.: Lost Highway, 2000).

11. Like all African-American folk-rural cultural traditions, Negro spirituals are tied to the King James Version of the Bible. The term *folk rural* comes from the cultural moments or categories devised by Richard Long in *African Americans* (New York: Random House, 1993, 9–19) to describe the African-American experience in the United States.

12. Biblical scholar Richard Cassidy sees Luke's emphasis on the poor as a theme throughout the entire gospel. See Richard J. Cassidy,

Jesus, Politics, and Society: A Study of Luke's Gospel (Maryknoll, N.Y.: Orbis, 1978).

13. The story of the rich man and Lazarus comes from the source that is Luke's special material, distinct from his use of Mark and from the source he shared with Matthew. In that special source, "Luke has a theme of riches and poverty. He appears to favor the poor" (Robert F. O'Toole, "Luke's Position on Politics and Society in Luke-Acts," in Richard J. Cassidy and Philip J. Scharper, eds., *Political Issues in Luke–Acts* [Maryknoll, N.Y.: Orbis Books, 1983], 11).

14. Cassidy, *Jesus, Politics, and Society*, 21.

15. Thinking about this text in terms of women at the gate was actually inspired by my reading novels by Francine Rivers and Obery Hendricks. These novels fill in a missing anthropology of women that one needs in order to interpret the admonition against divorce. Once one grasps the really desperate situations created for women because of the power of men to divorce them arbitrarily, the justice issues of divorce become evident and the discussion on divorce no longer seems like an insertion in the text or an unrelated fragment. The elders in the gate often exercised the power to dispense justice. The concerns of the prophets for injustice in the marketplace become relevant with reference to women. When a man divorced a woman, he was placing her in a vulnerable and impoverished position in the marketplace; and when a man married a divorced woman, he was probably taking unjust advantage of an injustice imposing conditions on a woman unable to negotiate a just marriage contract. It was all part of what God found abominable. See Obery Hendricks, *Living Water* (New York: HarperCollins, 2004); Francine Rivers, *Unashamed* (Wheaton, Illinois: Tyndale, 2000); *Unshaken* (Wheaton, Illinois: Tyndale, 2001); *Unveiled* (Wheaton, Illinois: Tyndale, 2000); *Unspoken* (Wheaton, Illinois: Tyndale, 2001); and *Unafraid* (Wheaton, Illinois: Tyndale, 2001).

16. O'Toole, "Luke's Position on Politics," 12.

17. Charles Talbert (*Reading Luke: A Literary and Theological Commentary on the Third Gospel* [New York: Crossroad, 1986], 57) points out that

This is the only parable of Jesus that names a character. The name, Lazarus (he whom God helps), is symbolic of the beggar's piety. Moreover, ritual uncleanness is no evidence against piety (the unclean dogs who licked his sores rendered him unclean, from a pharisaic perspective). . . . A parable that portrayed its hero as an unclean beggar must have been as startling to Pharisaic assumptions (clean plus rich equals righteous) as one that depicted a Samaritan as a hero.

18. Jim Wallis, *God's Politics: Why the Right Gets It Wrong and the Left Doesn't Get It* (San Francisco: HarperCollins, 2005), xix.

19. Ibid.
20. Ibid., xv.
21. Ibid., xvii.

II. A Postcolonial Reading

1. Barbara E. Rowe, review of Kwok Pui-lan, *Discovering the Bible in the Non-Biblical World, Catholic Biblical Quarterly* 59 (1997): 382–83.

2. Timothy A. Lenchak, review of Kwok Pui-lan, *Discovering the Bible in the Non-Biblical World, Missiology* 25 (1997): 99.

3. Yeo Khiok-Khng, ed., *Navigating Romans through Cultures: Challenging Readings by Charting a New Course* (New York: T. & T. Clark International, 2004).

4. See http://img.photobucket.com/albums/v331/minjagur/new_map.jpg.

5. John Macgowan, *How England Saved China* (London: T. Fisher Unwin, 1913).

6. *Boston Globe*, 7 November 2004.

7. Kwok Pui-lan, "Discovering the Bible in the Non-Biblical World," *Semeia* (1989): 26–30.

8. Bill Aschroft, Gareth Griffiths, and Helen Tiffin, *The Empire Writes Back: Theory and Practice in Post-colonial Literatures*, 2nd ed. (London: Routledge, 2002), 219.

9. Joe Lockard, "The Star of Ljubljana," a review of Slavoj Zizek, *Iraq: The Borrowed Kettle, Tikkun*, January/February 2005, 72.

10. David Harvey, *The New Imperialism* (New York: Oxford University Press, 2003).

11. Noam Chomsky, *Hegemony or Survival: America's Quest for Global Dominance* (New York: Metropolitan Books, 2003), 11.

12. L. William Countryman, "The Bible, Heterosexism, and the American Public Discussion of Sexual Orientation," in *God Forbid: Religion and Sex in American Public Life*, Kathleen M. Sands, ed. (New York: Oxford University Press, 2000), 167.

13. Ibid., 169.

14. See the Web site for "Lift Every Voice!" http://www.everyvoice .org/lev/modules.php?name=News&file=article&sid=4.

15. Susanne Scholz, "Sodom and Gomorrah (Genesis 19:1-29) on the Internet: The Implications of the Internet for the Study of the Bible," in *Biblical Studies Alternatively: An Introductory Reader*, Susanne Scholz, comp. (Upper Saddle River, N.J.: Prentice Hall, 2003), 137–53.

16. Robert S. Fortner, "Digital Media as Cultural Metaphor," in *New Paradigms for Bible Study: The Bible in the Third Millennium*, Robert M. Fowler, Edith Blumhofer, and Fernando F. Segovia, eds. (New York: T. & T. Clark International, 2004), 45.

17. See Elisabeth Schüssler Fiorenza, *Rhetoric and Ethic: The Politics of Biblical Studies* (Minneapolis: Fortress Press, 1999), 44–46.

18. Ibid., 121–22.

19. Kathleen M. Sands, "Introduction," in *God Forbid*, 7.

20. Jim Wallis appeared on NBC News' "Meet the Press" on 28 November 2004. The transcript can be found at http://www.msnbc.msn .com/id/6601018.

21. Michel Foucault, *History of Sexuality* (New York: Vintage Books, 1985). Originally published in French in 1976.

22. Edward W. Said, *Culture and Imperialism* (New York: Alfred A. Knopf, 1994), 80–97.

23. Toni Morrison, *Beloved: A Novel* (New York: Alfred A. Knopf, 1998).

24. Delores S. Williams, *Sisters in the Wilderness: The Challenge of Womanist God-Talk* (Maryknoll, N.Y.: Orbis Books, 1993).

25. See especially the womanist contributions in *Festschrift for Delores S. Williams*, Union Seminary Quarterly Review 58, no. 3–4 (2004).

26. Homi Bhabha, ed., *Nation and Narration* (London: Routledge, 1990).

27. Renee K. Harrison, "Hagar Ain't Workin', Gimme Me Celie: A Hermeneutic of Rejection and a Risk of Re-appropriation," *Union Seminary Quarterly Review* 58, no. 3–4 (2004): 45.

28. Clifford Longley, *Chosen People: The Big Idea that Shaped England and America* (London: Hodder and Stoughton, 2002), ix–x.

29. Delores S. Williams, "The Color of Feminism: Or Speaking the Black Women's Tongue," *Journal of Religious Thought* 43:1 (1986): 42–58.

30. Gale A. Yee, *Poor Banished Children of Eve: Woman as Evil in the Hebrew Bible* (Minneapolis: Fortress Press, 2003), 1.

31. Ibid., 159.

32. Ibid., 24.

33. Ibid., 59–79.

34. Marcella Althaus-Reid, *Indecent Theology: Theological Perversions in Sex, Gender, and Politics* (London: Routledge, 2001).

35. Ibid., 37–46.

36. John C. Hutchison, "Women, Gentiles, and the Messianic Mission in Matthew's Genealogy," *Bibliotheca Sacra* 158 (2001): 154–55.

37. Raymond Brown, *The Birth of the Messiah* (Garden City, N.Y.: Doubleday, 1977), 74.

38. Phyllis A. Bird, "The Harlot as Heroine: Narrative Art and Social Presupposition in Three Old Testament Texts," in Bird, *Missing Persons and Mistaken Identities: Women and Gender in Ancient Israel* (Minneapolis: Fortress Press, 1997), 215.

39. Ibid.

40. Danna Nolan Fewell and David M. Gunn, *Gender, Power, and Promise: The Subject of the Bible's First Story* (Nashville, Tenn.: Abingdon, 1993), 121.

41. Laura E. Donaldson, "The Sign of Orpah: Reading Ruth through Native Eyes," in *Vernacular Hermeneutics*, R. S. Sugirtharajah, ed. (Sheffield, UK: Sheffield Academic Press, 1999), 30.

42. Lori L. Rowlett, "Disney's Pocahontas and Joshua's Rahab in Postcolonial Perspective," in *Culture, Entertainment and the Bible*, George Aichele, ed. (Sheffield, UK: Sheffield Academic Press, 2000), 67.

43. Ibid., 68.

44. Ibid.

45. Musa W. Dube, *Postcolonial Feminist Interpretation of the Bible* (St. Louis, Mo.: Chalice, 2000), 129.

46. Ibid., 76.

47. Ibid., 77.

48. Ibid., 80.

49. Denise Brennen, "Selling Sex for Visas: Sex Tourism as a Stepping-stone to International Migration," in *Global Women: Nannies, Maids, and Sex Workers in the New Economy*, Barbara Ehrenreich and Arlie Russell Hochschild, eds. (New York: Metropolitan Books, 2002), 156.

50. Nantawan Boonprasat Lewis, "Remembering Conquest: Religion, Colonization, and Sexual Violence: A Thai Experience," in *Remembering Conquest: Feminist/Womanist Perspectives on Religion, Colonization, and Sexual Violence*, Nantawan Boonprasat Lewis and Marie M. Fortune, eds. (New York: Haworth Pastoral Press, 1999), 7–8.

51. Rita Nakashima Brock and Susan Brooks Thistlewaite, *Casting Stones: Prostitution and Liberation in Asia and the United States* (Minneapolis: Fortress Press, 1996), 76.

52. Albert Memmi, *The Colonizer and the Colonized* (Boston: Beacon, 1967).

53. Ashis Nandy, *The Intimate Enemy: Loss and Recovery of Self in Colonialism* (New Delhi, India: Oxford University Press, 1983).

54. Murray L. Newman, "Rahab and the Conquest," in *Understanding the Word: Essays in Honor of Bernhard W. Anderson*, James T. Butler, Edgar W. Conrad, and Ben C. Ollenburger, eds. (Sheffield, UK: Sheffield Academic Press, 1985), 174.

55. Rowlett, "Disney's Pocahontas and Joshua's Rahab," 75.

56. See the discussion in Victor Paul Furnish, "The Bible and Homosexuality: Reading the Texts in Context," in *Homosexuality in the Church: Both Sides of the Debate*, Jeffrey S. Siker, ed. (Louisville, Ky.: Westminster/John Knox, 1994), 18–35.

57. Robert Goss, *Jesus Acted Up: A Gay and Lesbian Manifesto* (San Francisco: HarperSanFrancisco, 1993), 90. Goss borrows the phrase "texts of terror" from Phyllis Trible.

58. Richard Horsley, ed., *Paul and Empire: Religion and Power in Roman Imperial Society* (Harrisburg, Pa.: Trinity Press International, 1997*)*; *Paul and Politics: Ekklesia, Israel, Imperium, Interpretation* (Harrisburg, Pa.: Trinity Press International, 2000); *Paul and the Roman Imperial Order* (Harrisburg, Pa.: Trinity Press International, 2004).

59. Horsley, "Introduction," *Paul and the Roman Imperial Order*, 3.

60. See, for example, Elisabeth Schüssler Fiorenza, "Paul and the Politics of Interpretation," in *Paul and Politics*, 40–57; Cynthia Briggs Kittredge, "Corinthian Women Prophets and Paul's Argumentation in 1 Corinthians," in ibid., 103–23.

61. Uma Narayan, *Dislocating Cultures: Identities, Traditions, and Third World Women* (New York: Routledge, 1997), 1–39; Robert J. C. Young, *Postcolonialism: A Historical Introduction* (Oxford: Blackwell, 2001), 360–82.

62. Bernadette J. Brooten, *Love between Women: Early Christian Responses to Female Homoeroticism* (Chicago: University of Chicago Press, 1996), 9–14.

63. Mary Rose D'Angelo, "Early Christian Sexual Politics and Roman Imperial Family Values: Reading Christ and Culture," in *The Papers of the Henry Luce III Fellows in Theology*, vol. 6, Christopher I. Wilkins, ed. (Pittsburgh: Association of Theological Schools, 1993), 23–48; D'Angelo, "'Knowing How to Preside over His Own Household': Imperial Masculinity and Christian Asceticism in the Pastorals, *Hermas*, and Luke-Acts," in *New Testament Masculinities*, Stephen D. Moore and Janice Capel Anderson, eds. (Atlanta: Society of Biblical Literature, 2003), 265–95.

64. See the discussion in Goss, *Queering Christ* (Cleveland: Pilgrim, 2002), 200.

65. Brooten, *Love between Women*, 272–80.

66. Ibid., 216.

67. L. William Countryman, *Dirt, Greed, and Sex: Sexual Ethics in the New Testament and Their Implications for Today* (Philadelphia: Fortress Press, 1988), 117.

68. Dale B. Martin, "Heterosexism and the Interpretation of Romans 1:18-32," *Biblical Interpretation* 3 (1995): 334–35.

69. Goss, *Jesus Acted Up*, 92–93.

70. Schüssler Fiorenza, "Paul and the Politics of Interpretation," 46-47.

71. Jennifer Wright Knust, "Paul and the Politics of Virtue and Vice," in *Paul and the Roman Imperial Order*, Richard A. Horsley, ed. (Harrisburg, Pa.: Trinity Press International, 2004), 173.

72. Homi K. Bhabha, *The Location of Culture* (London: Routledge, 1994), 114.

73. Janet R. Jakobsen, "Why Sexual Regulation? Family Values and Social Movements," in *God Forbid*, 112.

III. A Communal Reading

1. Justo L. González, *Tres Meses en La Escuela de la Patmos: Estudios Sobre el Apocalipsis* (Nashville, Abingdon, 1997), 2–4.

2. Virgilio P. Elizondo, *Galilean Journey*, rev. and expanded ed. (New York: Orbis Books, 2005), 43.

3. An established church assumes all financial responsibility, while a mission is sustained by a conference and/or a general agency.

4. Phillip Jenkins, *The Next Christendom: the Coming of Global Christianity* (New York: Oxford, 2002), 101–102.

5. David T. Abalos, *Latinos in the United States: The Sacred and the Political* (Notre Dame, Ind.: Notre Dame Press, 1986), 98.

6. Ibid., 98.

7. Abalos, *The Latino Family and the Politics of Transformation* (Westport, Conn.: Praeger, 1994), xix.

8. Mary Ann Tolbert, "Mark," in *The Women's Bible Commentary*, Carol A. Newsom and Sharon H. Ringe, eds. (expanded ed.; Louisville, Ky.: Westminster/John Knox, 1998); Pheme Perkins, "The Gospel of Mark, in *The New Interpreter's Bible*, Vol. 8 (Nashville, Tenn.: Abingdon, 1995); Choon-Leong Seow, "The First and Second Books of Kings," in ibid., 3:1–295.

9. David L. Petersen, "Introduction to Prophetic Literature," vol. 6 *The New Interpreter's Bible* (Nashville: Abingdon, 1995), 4–5.

10. Eugene H. Peterson, *The Message: The New Testament, Psalms, and Proverbs* (Colorado: NAVPRESS, 1995), 492.

Other Resources

Darr, Katheryn Pfisterer. "The Book of Ezekiel: Commentary and Reflections," vol. 6, *The New Interpreter's Bible*. Nashville, TN: Abingdon, 1995.

Elizondo, Virgilio P. *Galilean Journey*, rev. expanded ed. (New York: Orbis, 2005).

———. *Latinos in the United States: the Sacred and the Political.* Notre Dame, Ind.: Notre Dame Press, 1986.

Trinidad, Saul. *Modulo I: Programa de Capacitación para el Desarrollo de Ministerios Hispanos.* Nashville, Tenn.: Discipleship Resources, 2002.

IV. A Critical Feminist Emancipative Reading

1. See, for example Janice Capel Anderson, "Mapping Feminist Biblical Criticism," *Critical Review of Books in Religion* 2 (1991):

21–44; Elizabeth Castelli, "Heteroglossia, Hermeneutics and History: A Review Essay of Recent Feminist Studies of Early Christianity," *The Journal of Feminist Studies in Religion* 10/2 (1994): 73–8; Luise Schottroff, S. Schroer, and M.T. Wacker, eds., *Feminist Interpretation: The Bible in Women's Perspective* (Minneapolis: Fortress Press, 1998); Musa W. Dube, ed., *Other Ways of Reading: African Wo/men and the Bible* (Atlanta: Scholars Press, 2002); Silvia Schroer and Sophia Bietenhard, eds., *Feminist Interpretation of the Bible and the Hermeneutics of Liberation* (New York: Sheffield, 2003). For Jewish feminist interpretations, see the work of Esther Fuchs, Ilana Pardes, Adele Reinhartz, Tal Ilan, Amy Jill Levine, Cynthia Baker, Alicia Suskin Ostriker, and many others. See also Esther Fuchs, "Points of Resonance," in *On the Cutting Edge*, Jane Schaberg, Alice Bach, and Esther Fuchs, eds. (New York: Continuum, 2004), 1–20. For Muslim feminist hermeneutics, see, for example, Amina Wadud, *Qur'an and Woman: Rereading the Sacred Text from a Woman's Perspective* (Oxford: Oxford University Press, 1999); Barbara F. Stowasser, *Women in the Qur'an: Traditions and Interpretations* (New York: Oxford University Press, 1994); Asma Barlas, "Believing Women," in *Islam: Unreading Patriarchal Interpretations of the Qur'an* (Austin, Tex.: University of Texas, 2002).

2. See also my contribution in Ann Braude, ed., *Transforming the Faith of Our Fathers* (New York: Palgrave, 2004), 135–56, and my article, "Claiming the Power of the Word: Charting Critical Global Feminist Biblical Studies," in Kathleen Wicker, Althea Spencer-Miller and Musa Dube, eds., *Feminist New Testament Studies: Global and Future Perspectives* (New York: Palgrave Macmillan, 2005), 43–62; Elisabeth Schüssler Fiorenza, ed., *Searching the Scriptures: A Feminist Introduction* (New York: Crossroad, 1993).

3. Elisabeth Schüssler Fiorenza, Katie G. Cannon, Jane Schaberg, and David Barr, "Pedagogy and Practice: Using Wisdom Ways in the Classroom," *Teaching Theology and Religion* 6 (2003): 208–10, 225–26. For such a process see also John Lanci, "To Teach Without a Net," in *Walk in the Ways of Wisdom: Essays in Honor of Elisabeth Schüssler Fiorenza*, Cynthia Briggs Kittredge, Melanie Johnson-Debaufre, and Shelly Matthews, eds. (Harrisburg, Pa.: Trinity Press International, 2003), 58–73. For feminist pedagogy, see Katie G. Cannon, Kelly Brown Douglas, Toinette M. Eugene, and Cheryl Townsend Gilkes, "Living It Out: Metalogues and Dialogues: Teaching the Womanist Idea," *Journal of Feminist Studies in Religion* 8, no. 2 (Fall) 1992: 125–52; Fawzia Ahmad, "Engaging a New Discourse: Teaching 'Women in Islam' in the American University Classroom," *Journal of Feminist Studies in Religion* 18, no. 2 (2002): 131–40; Amy Richlin, "Teaching Religion and Feminist Theory to a New Generation," in "Roundtable: Feminists and Religion," *Journal of Feminist Studies in Religion* 14, no. 2 (1998): 124–31; Rebecca S. Chopp, *Saving*

Work: Feminist Practices of Theological Education (Louisville, Ky.: Westminster/John Knox, 1995).

4. For the problematic meaning of the term *woman/women* see Denise Riley, *"Am I That Name": Feminism and the Category of Women in History* (Minneapolis: University of Minnesota Press, 1988); Judith Butler, *Gender Trouble: Feminism and the Subversion of Identity* (New York: Routledge, 1990).

5. I coined the neologism *kyriarchy*, derived from the Greek words for "lord" or "master" (*kyrios*) and "to rule or dominate" (*archein*), in order to redefine the analytic category of *patriarchy* in terms of multiplicative intersecting structures of domination. Kyriarchy is a sociopolitical system of domination in which elite, educated, propertied men hold power over wo/men. Kyriarchy is best theorized as a complex pyramidal system of intersecting multiplicative social structures of supremacy and subordination, of ruling and oppression.

6. *Kyriocentrism* is a name for the linguistic-cultural-religious-ideological systems and intersecting discourses of race, gender, heterosexuality, class, imperialism, and other dehumanizing discourses that legitimate, inculcate, and sustain kyriarchy—that is, multiple structures of domination.

7. See, for example, R. S. Sugirtharajah, ed., *The Postcolonial Bible* (Sheffield, UK: Sheffield Academic Press, 1998).

8. Paolo Freire, *Pedagogy of the Oppressed* (New York: Seabury, 1973), 31. Freire is still very important, although his androcentric blinders have been pointed to, and his liberation discourse has gone out of vogue.

9. Ibid., 33.

10. See Elisabeth Schüssler Fiorenza, ed., *The Power of Naming: A Concilium Reader in Feminist Christian Theology* (Maryknoll, N.Y.: Orbis, 1996) and Elisabeth Schüssler Fiorenza and Shawn Copeland, eds., *Feminist Theologies in Different Contexts*, Concilium (Maryknoll, N.Y.: Orbis, 1996).

11. See also Sharon Welch, *Communities of Resistance and Solidarity* (Maryknoll, NY: Orbis), 7: ". . . the referent of the phrase 'liberating God' is not primarily God but liberation. That is the language here is true not because it corresponds with something in the divine nature but because it leads to actual liberation in history. The truth of God language and of all theological claims is measured . . . by the fulfillment of its claims in history."

12. In order to mark the inadequacy of our language about G*d, I had adopted the Jewish orthodox way of writing the name of *G-d* in my books *Discipleship of Equals* and *But She Said*. However, Jewish feminists have pointed out to me that such a spelling is offensive to many of them because it suggests a very conservative, if not reactionary, theological frame of reference. Hence I have begun to write the word *G*d* in this fashion in order to visibly destabilize our way of thinking and speaking about the Divine.

13. For the problem of translating grammatically gendered languages such as Greek or English into a non-gendered language system, see now the very interesting article of Satoko Yamaguchi, "Father Image of G*d and Inclusive Language: A Reflection in Japan," in *Toward a New Heaven and a New Earth: Essays in Honor of Elisabeth Schüssler Fiorenza*, Fernando F. Segovia, ed. (Maryknoll, N.Y.: Orbis Books, 2003), 199–224. I hope that this article will engender more research on biblical translation and interpretation in non-androcentric language contexts.

14. See the still very useful book by Brian Wren, *What Language Shall I Borrow? God-Talk in Worship: A Male Response to Feminist Theology* (New York: Crossroad, 1989).

15. See my discussion of anti-Judaism in "Feminist Interpretation," in *Jesus and the Politics of Interpretation* (New York: Continuum, 2000) 115–44; Amy Jill Levine, "Lilies of the Field and Wandering Jews: Biblical Scholarship, Wo/men's Roles, and Social Location," in Ingrid Rosa Kitzberger, ed., *Transformative Encounters. Jesus and Wo/men Re-Viewed* (Leiden, Netherlands: Brill, 2000), 328–52, and the Roundtable Discussion "Anti-Judaism and Postcolonial Biblical Interpretation," *Journal of Feminist Studies in Religion* 20, no. 1 (2004): 91-132.

16. Judith Fetterly, *The Resisting Reader: A Feminist Approach to American Fiction* (Bloomington: Indiana University Press, 1978).

17. For my theoretical argument and its exemplification on Pauline texts, see my book *Rhetoric and Ethic: The Politics of Biblical Studies* (Minneapolis: Fortress Press, 1999).

18. Severino Croatto, *Biblical Hermeneutics: Toward a Theory of Reading as the Production of Meaning* (Maryknoll, N.Y.: Orbis Books, 1987), 80: ". . . the hermeneutics of a text is conditioned by the text itself. The text indicates the limits (however broad) of its own meaning. A text *says what it permits to be said*. Its polysemy arises from its previous *closure*. Hence, the urgency of situating it in its proper context, by means of historical-critical methods, and of exploring its capacity for the production of meaning (according to the laws of semiotics), in order thus to cause its 'forward' to blossom from within life" (emphasis in original).

19. Elisabeth Schüssler Fiorenza, *In Memory of Her: A Feminist Theological Reconstruction of Christian Origins* (New York: Crossroad, 1983; Tenth Anniversary Edition, 1994; 2nd edition, London: SCM Press, 1995).

20. *Bread Not Stone: The Challenge of Feminist Biblical Interpretation* (Boston: Beacon, 1985; Tenth Anniversary Edition, 1995).

21. *But She Said: Feminist Practices of Biblical Interpretation* (Boston: Beacon, 1992).

22. *Sharing Her Word: Feminist Biblical Interpretation in Context* (Boston: Beacon, 1998).

23. *Wisdom Ways: Introducing Feminist Biblical Interpretation* (Maryknoll, NY: Orbis, 2001).

24. See especially *But She Said*, 51–76 and 195–218, for the elaboration of this process with reference to a particular text.

25. For such a hermeneutical reading see Sandra Marie Schneiders, *The Revelatory Text: Interpreting the New Testament as Sacred Scripture* (New York: HarperSanFrancisco, 1991).

26. For a similar theoretical framework see bell hooks, *Feminist Theory: From Margin to Center* (Boston: South End Press, 1984).

27. For a perceptive discussion of the *ekklesia of wo/men* see Elizabeth Castelli, "The Ekklēsia of Women and/as an Utopian Space: Locating the Work of Elisabeth Schüssler Fiorenza in Feminist Utopian Thought," in *On the Cutting Edge*, ed. Jane Schaberg, Alice Bach, and Esther Fuchs (New York: Continuum, 2004), 21-35; see also the discussion by Jánnine Jobling, *Feminist Biblical Interpretation in Theological Context* (Burlington: Ashgate, 2002).

28. See *In Memory of Her* for this concept.

29. See Elisabeth Schüssler Fiorenza, "Re-Visioning Christian Origins: *In Memory of Her* Revisited," in *Christian Beginnings: Worship, Belief and Society*, Kieran O'Mahony, ed. (London: Continuum International, 2003), 225-50.

30. "(2:9) But you are a chosen race, a royal priesthood, a holy nation, God's own people, in order that you may proclaim the mighty acts of him who called you out of darkness into his marvelous light. (2:10) Once you were not a people, but now you are God's people; once you had not received mercy, but now you have received mercy. (2:11) Beloved, I urge you as aliens and exiles to abstain from the desires of the flesh that wage war against the soul. (2:12) Conduct yourselves honorably among the Gentiles, so that, though they malign you as evildoers, they may see your honorable deeds and glorify God when he comes to judge.

"(2:13) For the Lord's sake accept the authority of every human institution, whether of the emperor as supreme, (2:14) or of governors, as sent by him to punish those who do wrong and to praise those who do right. (2:15) For it is God's will that by doing right you should silence the ignorance of the foolish. (2:16) As servants of God, live as free people, yet do not use your freedom as a pretext for evil. (2:17) Honor everyone. Love the family of believers. Fear God. Honor the emperor.

"(2:18) Slaves, accept the authority of your masters with all deference, not only those who are kind and gentle but also those who are harsh. (2:19) For it is a credit to you if, being aware of God, you endure pain while suffering unjustly. (2:20) If you endure when you are beaten for doing wrong, what credit is that? But if you endure when you do right and suffer for it, you have God's approval. (2:21) For to this you have been called, because Christ also suffered for you, leaving you an example, so that you should follow in his steps. (2:22) "He committed no sin, and no deceit was found in his mouth." (2:23) When he was abused, he did not return abuse; when he suffered, he did not threaten; but he entrusted himself to the one who judges justly. (2:24) He himself bore our sins in his body on the cross, so that, free from sins, we might live for righteousness; by his wounds you have been healed. (2:25) For you were going astray like sheep, but now you have returned to the shepherd and guardian of your souls.

"(3:1) Wives, in the same way, accept the authority of your husbands, so that, even if some of them do not obey the word, they may be won over without a word by their wives' conduct, (3:2) when they see the purity and reverence of your lives. (3:3) Do not adorn yourselves outwardly by braiding your hair, and by wearing gold ornaments or fine clothing; (3:4) rather, let your adornment be the inner self with the lasting beauty of a gentle and quiet spirit, which is very precious in God's sight. (3:5) It was in this way long ago that the holy women who hoped in God used to adorn themselves by accepting the authority of their husbands. (3:6) Thus Sarah obeyed Abraham and called him lord. You have become her daughters as long as you do what is good and never let fears alarm you. (3:7) Husbands, in the same way, show consideration for your wives in your life together, paying honor to the woman as the weaker sex, since they too are also heirs of the gracious gift of life—so that nothing may hinder your prayers." (NRSV)

31. See Kathleen Corley, "1 Peter," in Elisabeth Schüssler Fiorenza, ed., *Searching the Scriptures: A Feminist Commentary* (New York: Crossroad, 1994), 349-60, and my essay "Empire and Subordination: A Critical Feminist Postcolonial Commentary to 1 Peter," in Fernando Segovia and R.S. Sugirtharajah, eds., *A Postcolonial New Testament Commentary* (New York: Trinity Press, forthcoming).

32. David L. Balch, *Let Wives be Submissive: The Domestic Code in 1 Peter*, Society of Biblical Literature Monograph Series 26 (Chico: Scholars Press, 1981); John H. Elliott, *A Home for the Homeless: A Sociological Exegesis of 1 Peter, Its Situation and Strategy* (Philadelphia: Fortress Press, 1981); see also Klaus Thraede, "Zum historischen Hintergrund der 'Haustafeln' des NT," *Jahrbuch für Antike und Christentum, Ergänzungsband* 8 (1981): 359-68; Kathleen O'Brien Wicker, "First Century Marriage Ethics: A Comparative Study of the House-hold Codes and Plutarch's Conjugal Precepts," in James Flanagan and Anita W. Robinson, eds., *No Famine in the Land* (Missoula, Mont.: Scholars Press, 1975), 141-53; David Balch, "Household Ethical Codes in Peripatetic, Neopythagorean, and Early Christian Moralists," in Paul J. Achtemeier, ed., *Society of Biblical Literature Seminar Papers II* (Missoula, Mont.: Scholars Press, 1977), 397-404.

33. Barth L. Campbell, *Honor, Shame, and The Rhetoric of 1 Peter*, Society of Biblical Literature Dissertation Series 160 (Atlanta: Scholars, 1998).

34. John H. Elliott, "Disgraced Yet Graced: The Gospel according to 1 Peter in the Key of Honor and Shame," *Biblical Theology Bulletin* 24 (1994) 166–78.

35. Steven Richter Bechtler, *Following in His Steps: Suffering, Community, and Christology in 1 Peter*, Society of Biblical Literature Dissertation Series 162 (Atlanta: Scholars, 1998).

36. See, for example, M. Eugene Boring, *1 Peter*, Abingdon New Testament Commentaries (Nashville, Tenn.: Abingdon, 1999).

37. John H. Elliott, *1 Peter: A New Translation with Introduction and Commentary*, The Anchor Bible (New York: Doubleday, 2000); Paul J. Achtemeier, *1 Peter*, Hermeneia (Minneapolis: Fortress Press, 1996).

38. Toni Morrison, *Beloved* (New York: Knopf, 1987), 88.

39. Regula Strobel, "Brot nicht Steine," *Fama* 14/2 (1998), 11 (my translation).

40. See Elisabeth Schüssler Fiorenza and Kwok Pui-lan, eds., *Women's Sacred Scriptures*, Concilium (Maryknoll, N.Y.: Orbis, 1998).

V. A Critical Relational Reading

1. Marc H. Ellis, *Unholy Alliance: Religion and Atrocity in Our Time* (Minneapolis: Fortress Press, 1997), 177.

2. All biblical quotations are taken from the NSRV.

3. John Dominic Crossan, "Loosely Based on a True Story: The Passion of Jesus Christ in Verbal and Visual Media," *Tikkun* 19, no. 2 (2004): 27.

4. Ellis, *Unholy Alliance*, 193.

5. Irshad Manji, *The Trouble with Islam: A Muslim's Call for Reform in Her Faith* (New York: St. Martin's, 2003), 47.

6. Gustavo Gutiérrez, *A Theology of Liberation* (Maryknoll, N.Y.: Orbis, 1973).

7. Delores S. Williams, *Sisters in the Wilderness: The Challenge of Womanist God-Talk* (Maryknoll, N.Y.: Orbis, 1993).

8. This is a basic theme in Mary Hunt's *Fierce Tenderness: A Feminist Theology of Friendship* (New York: Continuum, 1991).

9. Ibid., 174.

10. As cited by ibid., 149, 151, 160. See Adrienne Rich, *The Dream of a Common Language: Poems 1974–1977* (New York: Norton, 1978) 74–75; Joan Casañas, "The Task of Making God Exist," in *The Idols of Death and the God of Life: A Theology*, Pablo Richard, ed., Barbara Campbell and Bonnie Shepherd, trans. (Maryknoll, N.Y.: Orbis, 1983), 141, 135, 138; Martin Buber, *Eclipse of God: Studies in the Relation Between Religion and Philosophy* (New York, NY: Harper & Row, 1952), 7–8.

11. Ellis, *Unholy Alliance*, 155.

12. The primary problem with the legacy that liberal Christians have received from Friedrich Schleiermacher is not so much his high view of human nature or even his focus on the individual (which I see as more of a problem), but rather his failure, and ours, to understand the *disruptive*

character of God. Schleiermacher was attempting to move nineteenth-century European Christians beyond their personal understandings of God into a religious experience deeper and broader than most Christians then or now can imagine. But Schleiermacher did not realize that "the feeling of absolute dependence" (which I would translate as an intuition of absolute interconnectedness, and hence relativity) is an opening to the *unknown*, which often involves an experience of God breaking into our lives and shaking us up. In other words, Schleiermacher did not realize—and his liberal Protestant heirs have not adequately comprehended—that Christian faith is not only a collective, relational journey taken by people who are sharing, indeed living, an intuition of absolute dependence upon God. As importantly, Christian faith is a journey that often involves disruption by the Spirit. Moreover, unless there is some in-breaking of the Spirit from beyond our realms of reference, our experiences of the Christian faith—including our interpretations of the Bible—will always be limited by what we bring to the experience: Our individual understandings of what we are doing, why we are doing it, and what it means to us. Without the intrusion of something from beyond our experiences, we are unable to chart new territories, because we do not know that there *are* "new territories," much less how to get there from here. See Friedrich Schleiermacher, *On Religion: Speeches to Its Cultured Despisers* (1799; New York: Harper Torchbooks, 1958).

13. Dorothee Soelle, *Creative Disobedience* (1968; Minneapolis: Fortress Press, 1995).

14. I first encountered the term "kin-dom" through conversations with *mujerista* theologian Ada María Isasi-Díaz in the 1980s.

15. Jay B. McDaniel, *Of God and Pelicans: A Theology of Reverence for Life* (Louisville, Ky.: Westminster/John Knox Press, 1989), 14.

16. Carter Heyward with Beverly Hall (photographer), *Flying Changes: Horses as Spiritual Teachers* (Cleveland, Ohio: Pilgrim, in press).

17. Ibid., 14.

18. Ibid., 50.

19. Carter Heyward, *Touching Our Strength: The Erotic as Power and the Love of God* (San Francisco: Harper and Row, 1993), 73–74.

20. Katie G. Cannon and Delores S. Williams articulated this in a meeting of The MudFlower Collective, to which we all belonged. See MudFlower Collective, *God's Fierce Whimsy: Christian Feminism and Theological Education* (Cleveland, Ohio: Pilgrim, 1985). See also Katie G. Cannon, *Black Womanist Ethics* (Atlanta: Scholars, 1988) and *Katie's Canon: Womanism and the Soul of the Black Community* (New York: Continuum, 1995), as well as Delores S. Williams, *Sisters in the Wilderness*.

21. Heyward, *Touching Our Strength*, 85.

Index

146

CPSIA information can be obtained at www.ICGtesting.com
Printed in the USA
LVOW05s0829181213

365702LV00004B/52/P